FOSSIL RIDGE PUBLIC LIBRARY DISTRICT

3 2186 00076 6401

W9-CBR-394

Fossil Ridge Public Library District
386 Kennedy Road
Braidwood, Illinois 60408

GAYLORD

THE SCANDINAVIAN AMERICAN

FAMILY ALBUM

THE SCANDINAVIAN AMERICAN
FAMILY
ALBUM

DOROTHY AND THOMAS HOOBLER
Introduction by Hubert H. Humphrey III

OXFORD UNIVERSITY PRESS • NEW YORK • OXFORD

FOSSIL RIDGE PUBLIC LIBRARY DISTRICT
Braidwood, IL 60408

Oxford University Press

Oxford New York
Athens Auckland Bangkok Bogotá Bombay
Buenos Aires Calcutta Cape Town Dar es Salaam
Delhi Florence Hong Kong Istanbul Karachi
Kuala Lumpur Madras Madrid Melbourne
Mexico City Nairobi Paris Singapore
Taipei Tokyo Toronto

and associated companies in
Berlin Ibadan

Copyright © 1997 by Dorothy and Thomas Hoobler
Introduction copyright © 1997 by Oxford University Press, Inc.

Design: Sandy Kaufman
Layout: Valerie Sauers
Consultant: Peter Kivisto, Associate Professor of Sociology, Augustana College

Published by Oxford University Press, Inc.,
198 Madison Avenue, New York, New York 10016

Oxford is a registered trademark of Oxford University Press

All rights reserved. No part of this publication
may be reproduced, stored in a retrieval system, or transmitted,
in any form or by any means, electronic, mechanical,
photocopying, recording, or otherwise, without the prior
permission of Oxford University Press.

Library of Congress Cataloging-in-Publication Data

Hoobler, Dorothy.
The Scandinavian American family album / Dorothy and Thomas Hoobler.
p. cm. — (American family albums)
Includes bibliographical references and index.
1. Scandinavian American families—History—Juvenile literature. 2. Scandinavian Americans—
History—Juvenile literature.
I. Hoobler, Thomas. II. Title. III. Series: Hoobler, Dorothy.
American family albums
E184.S18S64   1996
973'.04395—dc20   95-45540
                                                               CIP
                                                               AC

ISBN 0-19-510578-8 (lib. ed.); ISBN 0-19-510579-6 (trade ed.); ISBN 0-19-510172-3 (series, lib. ed.)

1 3 5 7 9 8 6 4 2

Printed in the United States of America
on acid-free paper

Cover: The interior of the Thorvald George Muller home in Kimballton, Iowa, around 1914. The grandfather clock at left had been in the Muller family since 1772 and was carried to the United States when the family emigrated from Denmark in 1884. The 12-year-old Thorvald carried one of its heavy weights in a gunnysack across the ocean.

Frontispiece: The Hedlund family celebrates the Fourth of July in St. Paul, Minnesota, in 1911.

CONTENTS

Introduction by Hubert H. Humphrey III ____ 6

CHAPTER ONE
THE OLD COUNTRIES _____ 9
Life in Scandinavia _____ 12
America Fever _____ 18

CHAPTER TWO
COMING TO THE UNITED
STATES _____ 23
Leaving Home _____ 26
Crossing the Ocean _____ 30
Scandinavians in Colonial America _____ 32

CHAPTER THREE
THE NEW LAND _____ 35
Arrival _____ 36
First Impressions _____ 40

CHAPTER FOUR
FINDING A JOB _____ 45
Forest and Sea _____ 48
Mining and Railroads _____ 54
Women's Work _____ 58
Farmers and Pioneers _____ 62
Factories and Unions _____ 72

CHAPTER FIVE
PUTTING DOWN ROOTS _____ 77
Communities _____ 80
Family _____ 90
School _____ 96
Religion _____ 100

CHAPTER SIX
PART OF THE UNITED
STATES _____ 105
Ties with the Homeland _____ 108
Preserving the Heritage _____ 112
The Esping Family _____ 118

Scandinavian American Timeline _____ 122
Further Reading _____ 123
Index _____ 126

INTRODUCTION

by Hubert H. Humphrey III

y family's voyage to America began with my paternal great-grandfather, Guttorn Andreas Sannes, who was a captain in the Norwegian Merchant Marine. He began as a cabin boy and worked his way up to captain, traveling to many distant and exciting lands, but his native homeland of Norway always held his heart captive.

Great-grandfather Sannes and his family lived on a farmstead just north of Kristiansand, Norway, where my grandmother was born. When my grandmother was three, the family left Norway for the sea. Raising a family on a ship was very trying, so my great-grandmother called an end to sea life. That's when my ancestors set off for the faraway land of America.

They eventually landed on the prairies of South Dakota. Though thousands of miles from an ocean, it was there that my great-grandfather hoped to be a captain again, this time aboard a riverboat on the Missouri River. Upon arriving in South Dakota, however, he found the river virtually unnavigable. But Norwegians like great-grandfather Sannes have great ingenuity and adaptability, and he turned to farming. He learned to love navigating a plow nearly as much as he loved navigating ships.

In my father's autobiography, he wrote that through good spirits and hope, his grandparents were determined "to live, not just survive." My great-grandparents believed that hard work and faith in God would provide for their family and, to this day, they are my role models for work and spirit. It was these people and their experience as immigrants that taught my grandmother, Christine Sannes Humphrey, as she grew up. My grandmother was my first real connection to Norway and what it meant to be Norwegian.

From my earliest days, I listened as my grandmother spoke Norwegian with friends and family, recalling stories told by her parents and remembering good times from her homeland. To her grandchildren, she told marvelous stories—tale after tale about Billy Goat Gruff, all the trolls, and Butterball. She would leave us scared to death of the stories, but we loved them. It was also through her stories that I learned about my Norwegian heritage and her struggles of being an immigrant child.

It was from my grandmother that my father received his wonderful gifts for storytelling—a trait that marked his political career. Politics, too, were part of my grandparents' day-to-day life.

Sunday dinners on the South Dakota Plains were always filled with good food and fiery political conversation. Sometimes the conversation would get so loud and heated, my grandmother would exclaim "Uff-da!" and return to the kitchen for some peace. She could only take so much of politics!

My parents went to Norway early during my father's career as a U.S. senator, and I can distinctly remember, as a little boy, being delighted when my mother brought back Norwegian trolls and traditional decorations for Christmas. In particular, I remember a small wooden Norwegian fishing boat they gave me, which even today reminds me of the stories about my great-grandfather, the sea captain.

My parents taught me what all Norwegians teach their children—that hard work and the values of family and honesty are what really matter in life. But the strongest Norwegian trait that passed through my family is determination—to go forward, without complaint, and to make the very best of what you have. It doesn't matter how cold it is, it doesn't matter whether you've got extra work to do, you just get the job done. That spirit came from my great-grandparents directly, and Norway indirectly.

Today, I see this Norwegian determination as I travel through

Daisy, Robert, Skip (Hubert Humphrey III), and Nancy enjoy skating with their parents, Muriel and Hubert Humphrey, in the 1950s.

Hubert H. Humphrey III was born in Minneapolis on June 26, 1942, the son of Muriel and Hubert H. Humphrey, Jr. Like his father, who served as a U.S. senator in the 1950s and as Vice President of the United States from 1965 to 1969, Humphrey has pursued a life in politics.

After graduating from American University and the University of Minnesota Law School, Humphrey served as a Minnesota state senator, practiced law, and worked as a deputy U.S. marshal in Washington, D.C. Since 1982 he has served as attorney general of Minnesota. Ad Week Magazine called him one of "The Ten Most Feared Attorneys General" in the nation for his efforts to stop corporate fraud and consumer rip-offs. He has devoted his time in office to fighting violent crime, designing programs to help children in need, and developing innovative environmental policies.

Humphrey and his wife, Nancy Lee, have three children: Lorie, Pamela, and Hubert Humphrey IV.

Minnesota, where many Norwegian immigrants settled and made their homesteads amid freezing winters and dry, hot summers. These children of immigrants often remind me of my heritage, as they argue politics over cup after cup of coffee.

I like to tell my children about their Scandinavian heritage because it shapes who they are and where they are going. This feeling has never overcome me more than when I visited my grandmother's birthplace in Kristiansand. I was overwhelmed by the beauty of the land, the history of the place, and the depth of commitment it must have taken for my great-grandparents to leave behind a life, family, friends, and language they knew, for a new country.

The story of my great-grandparents and grandparents is not only one of Norwegian immigrants, but really of all immigrants. My father grew up of modest means, in a small town that resembled hundreds of other little midwestern towns, and he became a U.S. senator, Vice President of the United States, and the Democratic candidate for President. His accomplishments are emblematic of what all immigrants can achieve.

Humphrey's grandparents, Hubert Humphrey, Sr., and Christine Sannes Humphrey, in Granite Falls, Minnesota, in 1910. They were married in April 1906 in Lily, South Dakota.

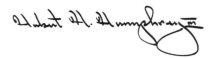

On August 24, 1996, in Minneapolis, Humphrey and his wife, Lee, join their daughters, Pamela (left) and Lorie (right), for a family portrait on the day of the wedding of their son, Hubert Humphrey IV, to Heidi Schadow.

7

Aukusti Kujala and Senja Kiviaho, an engaged couple, pose for a formal portrait in Finland in 1909.

CHAPTER ONE

THE OLD COUNTRIES

ext morning, Leif [Eriksson] said to his men, 'Now we have two tasks on our hands. On alternate days we must gather grapes and cut vines, and then fell trees to make a cargo for my ship.'

"This was done. It is said that the tow-boat was filled with grapes. They took on a full cargo of timber; and in the spring they made ready to leave and sailed away. Leif named the country after its natural qualities and called it *Vinland.*"

This is part of the *Graenlendinga Saga,* an ancient account of the first voyage by Norsemen to America, around the year 1000. Leif Eriksson's expedition was part of a great era of Norse exploration and migration. The Norsemen, or Nordic people, were the ancestors of today's Scandinavians, who live in Denmark, Finland, Iceland, Norway, and Sweden.

Norway and Sweden are located on a large peninsula north of the Baltic Sea. Across a narrow strait lies Denmark, which consists of several islands and Jutland, a peninsula on the mainland of Europe. The inhabitants of these three countries descend from Nordic peoples who migrated there at least 10,000 years ago.

Though winters were long in these northern lands, the Norse prospered by taking advantage of nature's bounty. They planted crops such as barley, oats, rye, peas, cabbage, and flax. Herders raised cattle, sheep, goats, and pigs.

The Scandinavian coasts are heavily indented with long inlets called *fjords*, which were carved out by glaciers during the last Ice Age. Fish from the seas and lakes, along with whales, walruses, and seals, were used for food, clothing, and oil. Women gathered wild berries, nuts, garlic, and leeks. The Norse also hunted reindeer, bears, rabbits, and ducks.

Nature provided everything necessary for life, and so the Norse worshiped a variety of nature gods. Festivals honoring the gods—usually with animal sacrifices and feasting—took place at midwinter, midsummer, and the autumn harvest.

The gods lived in Valhalla ("the hall of the slain"), where human heroes went after death. Odin, the chief god, had one eye; he had sacrificed the other to gain wisdom. But the ravens that flew through the skies reported everything they saw to him. Thor was the god of thunder, who ruled the winds and rains on which the crops depended. Frey, the god of fertility, was also a great warrior. His sister Freya was the goddess of love. From Odin, Thor, and Frey come the English words Wednesday, Thursday, and Friday.

The Finns are a people who originally lived in the area of the Ural Mountains. They moved into the southern part of today's Finland around the first century of the modern era. The Finns' language is very different from those of the other Scandinavian nations. Finland was divided into small tribal groups until it was absorbed by Sweden in the 13th century.

From the 8th to the 11th century, seafarers from today's Denmark, Norway, and Sweden began to sail away from their homelands. These "people of the *viks*" (their word for *fjord*) ventured forth in search of conquest and plunder. History knows them as the Vikings.

Norwegians and Danes went west, raiding villages in today's France, England, Ireland, and Wales. In their long, sturdy boats, they sailed up the Seine River to Paris, which they looted and burned. In time, Danish Vikings established a kingdom in England. Norwegians founded the city of Dublin on the east coast of Ireland.

The hardy Viking seafarers also ventured farther out on the Atlantic Ocean. Norwegians reached Iceland in the 9th century and established a colony there. Erik the Red, sailing from Iceland, reached Greenland around the year 980. (With the savvy of a modern real estate agent,

Erik gave the barren arctic island its appealing name to encourage more settlers to follow.)

Around the year 1000, Erik's son Leif missed Greenland on his way there from Iceland. Leif Eriksson and his crew reached America instead. Finding grapevines growing there, they called it Vinland. Modern scholars think Eriksson came ashore somewhere in Newfoundland.

Meanwhile, Vikings from today's Sweden were heading east and south. They crossed the Baltic Sea and established trading posts in southern Finland and today's Latvia, Lithuania, and Estonia.

In the early 9th century, the Swedes sailed into Lake Ladoga, in today's Russia. From there, they traveled south to the Volkhov and Dnieper rivers. The Slavs who lived in this area called the Vikings the Rus, probably from a word that means "seafarers."

According to legend, a Viking leader named Rurik gained control of the region between the river trading posts of Novgorod and Kiev. Kiev became the center of the first Russian state. Today, the city is the capital of Ukraine.

The Rus pushed south to the Black Sea. In the 9th and 10th centuries they attacked Constantinople, capital of the Byzantine Empire. Failing to take it, some of them entered the service of the empire as soldiers.

Farther east, other Vikings sailed down the Volga River and into the Caspian Sea. From there they made their way to Baghdad, where they traded with merchants from Arabia, India, and China.

Thus, in about three centuries, the Vikings had spread over an area

that stretched from North America to Asia. But there were too few of them to defend such a vast area. The Rus blended into the Slavic population of Russia. The Danish kingdom in England fell to William the Conqueror in 1066. (William himself was a descendant of Vikings who earlier had settled in Normandy.)

In the Vikings' homeland, kingdoms arose that formed the beginning of the modern Scandinavian nations. One ruler, Harald Fairhair, conquered other local chiefs and became king of Norway in 885. It was, in fact, Norwegians

A family gathering in front of a Norwegian farmhouse. The population grew faster in the 1800s than the food supply or the improvement in farming methods, and as a result, both fjord and mountain communities provided immigrants to America.

resisting Harald Fairhair's rule who first settled in Iceland.

During the next century, the Danes united into a kingdom under Svein Forkbeard, and Olaf Skautkonung became Sweden's first king in 993.

Near the end of 10th century, the kings of Denmark, Norway, and Sweden converted to Christianity. According to tradition, King Olaf of Norway (today Norway's patron saint) then went to Iceland to convert its inhabitants. The Icelandic Althing—today the world's oldest parliament—adopted the

faith around the year 1000. Christianity came to Finland in the 13th and 14th centuries, when the Swedes absorbed Finnish territory.

Today the people of Scandinavia are primarily Lutherans. The nations' flags reflect this Christian heritage. Though they are different colors, all five flags have the same pattern: a horizontal cross on a solid background.

Scandinavians have a long literary tradition as well. A form of writing known as runes appeared in Denmark in the 3rd century, and soon spread north to Norway and Sweden. The runes, which were inscribed on stones, swords, shields, and medallions, were partly based on the Greek and Latin alphabets. In their new Scandinavian form, they became associated with religious and magical ceremonies. Runic stones were also raised to commemorate important historical events. In outlying regions, use of the runes survived to modern times, although today's Scandinavians write their languages using the letters of the Western alphabet.

Aside from runic inscriptions, the oldest surviving Scandinavian literature comes from Iceland. The Icelandic *Eddas* are poems composed by *skaeds*, or poets, between the 9th and 13th centuries. Icelandic *skaeds* served as court poets throughout Scandinavia. Their works relate the myths and legends of heroes and gods.

Another form of ancient Scandinavian literature is the *Sagas*, prose stories that were first written down in the 13th century. A blend of fact and fantasy, the *Sagas* contain history and folktales about people who performed spectacular deeds. Like the *Eddas,* the *Sagas* were often recited by poets and storytellers to musical accompaniment.

The Finns, though conquered at different times by Swedes and Russians, struggled to preserve their distinct language. In 1835, when Finland was under the control of the Russian Empire, a scholar named Elias Lönnrot wrote Finland's national epic, the *Kalevala* (The Land of Heroes). Lönnrot assembled old tales and songs from oral tradition and used them to create this epic. One of its heroes is a supernatural being named Väinämöinen, a skilled singer and player of the *kantele,* the Finnish harp. He seeks to win the hand of the daughter of Louhi, the female ruler of a land farther north. Jean Sibelius (1865–1957), Finland's greatest composer, used the *Kalevala* as inspiration for some of his works.

The history of the Scandinavian countries has long been intertwined. Denmark, Norway, and Sweden became politically united in 1397 when Queen Margrethe of Denmark summoned nobles from the three countries to the city of Kalmar. They agreed to establish one united Scandinavian nation with Margrethe's son Eric as king. Iceland—then a part of Norway—and Finland, under Swedish rule, thus belonged to the union as well.

Sweden broke away from the Union of Kalmar in 1523, but Norway and Denmark remained one country until 1814. In that year, the victorious nations in the Napoleonic Wars met at the Congress of Vienna to redraw the map of Europe.

Sweden, one of the victors, was given control of Norway. (Denmark had been on the losing side.) Although the Norwegians staged a brief rebellion, the Swedish king ruled Norway and Sweden until 1905, when the two nations finally separated.

Another result of the Napoleonic Wars was that, in 1809, Finland became a grand duchy of the Russian Empire. In 1917, when the Russian Revolution began, the Finns took advantage of the situation to declare their independence. The Soviet Union, however, attacked Finland in 1940. During what was called the Winter War, the Finns hero-

The Andrew Johnsons, a Swedish family, sing and relax in front of their home. They lived in the southern part of Sweden on the Baltic coast. They emigrated in 1914 and settled in Tacoma, Washington.

ically defended their territory from their much larger neighbor.

In 1918, Iceland won recognition as a separate state under the king of Denmark. In 1944, the Icelandic Althing declared the nation an independent republic.

During the 19th century, a sizable proportion of the people from all the Scandinavian nations emigrated to the United States. Like immigrants from other nations, most of them were seeking economic opportunity. After about 1800, Scandinavia's population began to rise sharply. People found it

more and more difficult to find work, particularly in the rural areas.

Around 1840, "America fever" spread through Norway, the first Scandinavian country to lose large numbers of its people to the United States. A Norwegian living in the town of Snaasen described the excitement in those years: "For a time I believed that half of the population of Snaasen had lost their senses. Nothing else was spoken of but the land that flows with milk and honey. Our minister, Ole Rynning's father, tried to stop the fever. [Ole Rynning himself had emigrated and had written an enthusiastic guidebook for Norwegian immigrants.] Even from the pulpit he urged people to be discreet and described the hardships of the voyage...in the most forbidding colors. This was only pouring oil upon the fire."

America fever struck other Scandinavian nations not long afterward. The largest wave of immigration from Sweden and Denmark began in the 1860s. A decade later, Finns and Icelanders caught the fever. The immigrants from all five nations were mostly young people, eager to make better lives for themselves in a new country than they could at home.

In 1907, an official of the Swedish government reported that it was difficult "to find any farm where none of the immediate family are in America.... On the walls hang American group photographs of perhaps 15 or 20 relatives."

In the census of 1990, about 11.5 million Americans described themselves as being of Scandinavian descent. That is about half of the current population of the five nations from which they and their ancestors came.

During the 19th century, a large number of inhabitants of all five Scandinavian nations—Denmark, Finland, Iceland, Norway, and Sweden—left for America in search of economic opportunity.

Because summer is so short in the Scandinavian countries, people make the most of it. The midsummerfest, at the summer solstice, is a high point of the year. This is one Swedish family's summer cottage near Stockholm.

LIFE IN SCANDINAVIA

Jacob Riis was born in Ribe, Denmark, in 1849, the son of a schoolteacher. He came to the United States in 1870 and later became the founder of modern photojournalism. In his autobiography, he described his hometown.

In my day Ribe had...never changed a step of its ways since whale-oil lanterns first hung in iron chains across its cobblestone-paved streets to light them at night. There they hung yet, every rusty link squeaking dolefully in the wind that never ceased blowing from the sea. Coal-oil, just come from America, was regarded as a dangerous innovation. I remember buying a bottle of "Pennsylvania oil" at the grocer's for eight skilling [Danish coin], as a doubtful domestic experiment. Steel pens had not crowded out the old-fashioned goose-quill, and pen-knives meant just what their name implies. Matches were yet of the future. We carried tinderboxes to strike fire with. People shook their heads at the telegraph. The day of the stage-coach was not yet past....

Two or three times a year, usually in the fall, when it [the sea] blew long and hard from the northwest, it broke in over the low meadows and flooded the country as far as the eye could reach. Then the high causeways were the refuge of everything that lived in the fields; hares, mice, fox, and partridges huddled there, shivering in the shower of spray that shot over the road, and making such stand as they could against the fierce blast. If the "storm flood" came early in the season, before the cattle had been housed, there was a worse story to tell. Then the town butcher went upon the causeway at daybreak with the implements of his trade to save if possible, by letting the blood, at least the meat of drowned cattle and sheep that were cast up by the sea. When it rose higher and washed over the road, the mail-coach picked its way warily between white posts set on both sides to guide it safe. We boys caught fish in the streets of the town, while red tiles flew from the roofs all about us, and we enjoyed ourselves hugely. It was part of the duty of the watchmen who cried the hours to give warning if the sea came in suddenly during the night. And when we heard it we shivered in our beds with gruesome delight.

Aase Aslakson, born in 1863, came to the United States from Norway in 1879, at the age of 16. Years later she related her life as a young girl.

My parents were very poor, so, at the age of eight, I left home to make my own way in the world. I had to herd cattle and sheep and had very little schooling. I learned to write by drawing letters in the dirt with a long stick, while herding cattle....

Then came the time when I became a hired girl. This was a very hard place. I was up early in the morning and worked late into the night. It was my job to spin and weave and after dark the wool had to be carded. The coal had to be gathered in the woods. This was hard because we had to be up at night and watch the coal as it went through the burning process. For three hours every night I carried the water, then someone would come and take my place. I was so tired I slept with my clothes on even though they were covered with ice. While doing this work, I contracted asthma which bothers me to this day.

Thorstina Walters, the daughter of Icelandic immigrants, grew up in North Dakota. She remembered her grandfather describing conditions in Iceland in the second half of the 19th century.

Possibly the most entertaining of grandfather's stories, the ones he enjoyed telling more than any others, were connected with his boyhood days when he herded sheep followed by his faithful dog. He was constantly losing his flock in the fog that sneaked upon the shepherd before he was aware of its coming, so dark and impenetrable that even the dog seemed to lose his bearings. Grandfather went on to say that the general belief where he came from in Iceland was that the fog on the East Coast of the island was a Princess of wondrous beauty who was under a magic spell. Her only hope of release was through a youth who was a shepherd for seventeen years and never said anything against the fog. According to grandfather, no such patient shepherd had been found when he left Iceland, thus the poor Princess remained a dark, brooding fog over the landscape.

Axel Jarlson was born around 1880 in Sweden and came to the United States in 1899. He told an interviewer about his life in Sweden.

We were ten in the family, father and mother and eight children, and we had lived very happily in our cottage until the last year, when father and mother were both sick and we got into debt. Father had a little piece of land— about two acres—which he rented, and besides, he worked in the summer time for a farmer. Two of my sisters and three of my brothers also worked in the fields, but the pay was so very small that it was hard for us to get enough to eat. A good farm hand in our part of Sweden, which is 200 miles north of Stockholm and near the Baltic Sea, can earn about 100 kroner a season, and a kroner is 27 cents. But the winter is six months long, and most of that time the days are dark, except from ten o'clock in the morning to four o'clock in the afternoon. The only way our family could get money during the winter was by making something that could be sold in the market town, ten miles away. So my father and brothers did wood carving and cabinet making, and my mother and sisters knitted stockings, caps and mufflers and made homespun cloth, and also butter and cheese, for we owned two cows.

But the Swedish people who have money hold on to it very tight, and often we took things to market and then had to bring them home again, for no one would buy.

A street scene in Stavanger, Norway, in the early years of the 20th century. The first group of Norwegian immigrants left this port city for the United States in 1825. Throughout the 1800s, many more Norwegians from the area around Stavanger came to the United States.

The Icelanders had one of the highest rates of literacy in the world, and reading was the principal occupation for many during the long northern winter.

Isaac Polvi was born in Finland in 1878 and came to the United States 16 years later. As an old man, he wrote an autobiography in which he described conditions in the country he left.

There was not much money among us rural folk, and everything was paid for with labor. For example, the landowners had large holdings which they would develop into tenant farms by giving young couples permission to go into the backwoods of their land to build homes and make fields. They made a fifty-year contract which stipulated that every fourth week the tenant would work for the estate. This varied more or less with the kind of place the tenant farmer had built. But, in general, the young couples built the buildings, cleared off the forests and raised their families, while working every fourth or fifth week for the estate, according to the contract. This was what was called "taxes." There were not other land taxes.

The minister, however, collected what was called a "head tax." This tax was paid by all adults whether or not they owned property. I believe at the time it was one Finnish mark. But say you had cattle. Then you had to provide butter and milk, make cheese, and one-tenth of everything you grew belonged to the minister. The minister himself traveled about collecting these taxes....

It was told that when Isaac Kohtoola went to work to pay off the family's head taxes, the minister knew that he was someone with the skill to build a fish trap for use in the river. The fish swam into his traps and could be kept alive and free for weeks. When one wanted fresh fish one simply took a hoop-net and scooped out whatever amount was needed.

Isaac was working on such a trap for the minister but hadn't completed it after two days. The minister told him to go ahead and finish the job. "Surely," he added, "we can settle up afterwards."

Isaac knew that he would have difficulty settling his account. He had a pair of gloves which were made of thick cloth and were quite worn. He put them in a tar pot and left them there until he finished the trap. Then he would see whether or not the minister would pay him his wages, which in turn he

This Danish cooperative dairy farm was located on the Isle of Møn. In the second half of the 1800s, social reforms and advanced techniques made Denmark a leader in the dairy industry. Some Danish immigrants took their skills to America.

would use to pay his family's head taxes. So he finished the fish trap and then asked the minister to pay him his wages.

"Surely I can pay you later," said the minister while he greedily admired the splendid fish trap.

"Listen," said Isaac, "Let me tell you a thing or two. A devil-take-it bloodhead [a pike] won't enter that trap so long as you refuse to pay me my wages."

And with that Isaac collected his tools nearby, removed his old gloves from the tar pot, put one glove inside the other and placed them at the throat of the trap. Then following the minister's orders, he put the trap in the river. Naturally, the fish [detected] the odor of tar in the trap and turned away. So, when the minister went to get some fish there weren't any, and he began to believe. "Not even a hell-bound bloodhead will enter the trap so long as I don't pay Isaac his wages."

The minister went to Isaac and asked him, "Will fish go into the trap if I pay you for the two day's work I owe you?"

"If you pay me right now," said Isaac confidently, "there will be fish in the trap tomorrow morning."

Well, the minister paid, and Isaac went at dusk to the river and removed the tarred glove from the throat of the fish trap.

Ester Sundvik grew up on the Åland Islands, a province of Finland where many of the inhabitants are Swedish-speaking, as she was. She remembered what the holidays were like before she came to the United States in 1929.

Christmas was so beautiful at home and we had Christmas for twenty days. Every neighbor had a party. And we had our Christmas tree that we cut down from the woods, snow up to the waistline. We shook the snow out. We had a verandah that went across the whole house and mother used to keep it there and put paper under it so it wouldn't ruin the floor. Then when it was dry enough, we took it in and the whole house smelled from the fir. We didn't have any bought decorations. We made stars out of paper and little baskets of paper that were woven—slips of different kinds of paper, blue and green and red and all kinds—with a handle on it. Then we put a little candy or raisins or prunes in it, so the day the tree was taken down we could eat all those goodies. There were strips of colored paper that we made a garland out of and put around the tree. It was very cute when we got done with it. We had candleholders on the branches and we stuck candles in there, and we never had an accident or anything with the candles burning.

The first of May we had really big, big fires. We used to go up on the mountain and build the fires and then we could see all over town and all the church steeples. The mountain was not far from our house. We used to climb up there and make the fires and we used to sing *"Idag det förste maj, maj; idag det förste maj."* Today is the first of May.

Midsummer was also one of the highlights in our lives. They cut down birches and decorated the outside of the house with birch trees. Just at that time, the birch leaves were all out and they

The Hammerbak beer wagon delivered beer to stores throughout Copenhagen, Denmark. The girl on the pony is Elsie Hammerbak, who came to the United States in 1930.

In Iceland, farming is a difficult occupation because the growing season is short. By comparison, even the northern parts of the United States seemed attractive to the immigrants.

Ellen Peterson and Karin Lennstrom are dressed in costumes for a studio portrait. They wore these clothes to one of the public dances held in Stockholm in the early 1900s. Both women came to the United States within a few years.

The work was long and hard on the farms of Finland in the early years of the 1900s. Here, Sanna, Hilma, Hilja, and Kristiina Tunkkari churn butter in 1910.

were so pretty. Some people even made a little house with just birches all around it and then the entrance to go in; and there was a little table and you could go in there and have your coffee.

Henny Hale was born in Norway in 1903 and emigrated to the United States in 1923 on a ticket supplied by an uncle in Tacoma, Washington. Years later she recalled life in her homeland.

My father was a fisherman and a farmer. Father would go to Finnmarken [the northernmost district of Norway] in the late spring to fish, until he had to come back to work on his farm; and in the winter he went to the Lofoten Islands [prime fishing grounds off the northern coast of Norway] for cod. My mother died when she was thirty-six, leaving six children. She was a slender, pretty little thing, and she shouldn't have had to die so young. I remember her going down to the sea to get the heads of the fish and go home and boil them up and bring them to the barn for the cows. Mother used to crochet curtains and she had a loom and wove all the rugs for our floors. She was very handy. How she found time I don't know. Besides that, she was a seamstress and sewed for other people.

We used peat for heat; we had peat bogs all over the place. My dad would cut off about six thousand peat squares every spring; and we children had to slice these squares with a spade. That was heavy work. We with our little legs would stand there and slice up all these [squares] and then set them to dry. It was marvelous fuel. We had a *kamin* [stove] in the front room; it was very beautiful, with several tiers of iron where we could set coffee pots to warm.

After mother died, it was just me and my older sister that had to take over. I was twelve; my sister Mary was fourteen. We had to do the milking and the baking. Maybe I sound like we worked ourselves to death, well, we did. But that's how we lived up in the north; it was hard going. In the winter, now here was I, twelve years old, had to hack a road through the snow, hack holes in the river in the ice, carry about fourteen buckets every other day to the barn of the cows and the sheep. We had it to do and so we did it.

We took the sheep in from the barn and I clipped them in the kitchen. I was so short, I sat on the sheep's back and clipped

the wool off of it. There was a lady that used to come to the house all the time and I didn't like her. She was running after my dad when he was a widower. One time, I was clipping the wool of this sheep and she was sitting at the kitchen table having a cup of coffee. And I happened to clip the skin of the sheep and he didn't like it one bit, so the sheep leaped into that lady's lap and spilled her coffee and I was so glad. Isn't that terrible?

I was the tomboy. Mary was the lady. I ran out and played ball with the boys and went swimming in the river and I'd go fishing with my dad. Summer nights when he was home and the midnight sun was shining, we'd take the little boat and go way out and fill the bucket with little *gjedde* [pike]. We'd sit out on the water till the sun came to the sea and went up again [summer midnight sun, which only touches the horizon]. And then we'd go home and cook up a pot of that fish. We worked hard, but there were times when we enjoyed our life, too.

Martin Rasmussen was a Dane who grew up in what was called North Slesvig by the Germans, who occupied the region from 1864 until the German defeat in World War I. Rasmussen came to the United States in 1923 after serving in the German army during that war. Here, he told an interviewer about his early life.

My father had a nice farm. It was good-sized—a hundred and fifty acres or something like that, fourteen to eighteen cows, and six or seven horses. You had to work on the farm. You had to get the cows out in the field and everything in order before you went to school in the morning. Later on, you had to be out and pull up the rutabagas and turnips and so forth. We had some hired help, too.

Potatoes, we'd get a special vacation for potatoes, two weeks in September or August. Then the whole family was in the potato field; that was nasty and cold. Had a wonderful appetite when we got home at five or six o'clock. There was a couple of men digging; the rest of us were gathering the potatoes in sacks. In many cases, there was dug a big hole in the ground, the potatoes down there and straw on the bottom, and straw on the top, and dirt on it, and they would last all winter. There would be quite a few rotten ones, though. That was the same way with rutabagas—hauled to a hole and then covered up, but you didn't dig down as deep....

Going to church, menfolks sit on the one side and womenfolks sit on the other side. No mixed affairs, no. There was, like usual, singing, but no dancing. That was the Lutheran church....

For confirmation preparation you had to go there once a week, one forenoon each week for half a year. In the lectures for confirmation, we had to learn a lot of songs and to know about the Bible. Then for confirmation the boys had to stand on one side and the girls on the other side. The [congregation] was sitting in the pews and we were standing up there. He asked each one certain questions; I almost remember what he asked, it was something special from the New Testament. We had to answer and we'd better know the answer, too.

Thomas Tjøm (left) and his cousin, Thomas Tjøm Rennie, set lobster traps from their boat in southern Norway. Boys living on the coast learn early how to fish.

These Finnish sandals were woven from bark.

AMERICA FEVER

This "America letter" was written in Norwegian. In the home country, people with writing skills were in great demand to compose letters in reply.

Katrina ("Trina") Adamsen Hansen came from Denmark with her husband and parents in the 1860s. Her daughter, Inga Hansen Dickerson, retold the story of her mother's early years in Denmark.

Trina was nine. She lived on the island of Als, off the coast of Denmark, in a tiny thatched-roofed cottage with her parents. It was her task, while her parents were away working for the big landowner, to take care of her brother Anders, who was three, and to care for the family goat. As she tended to her duties, she used to watch the beautiful billowing clouds as they tumbled in the sky overhead, their shifting white display against the blue sky, making lovely patterns...white sails...drifting beyond the unknown horizon to begin their trek hither and yon...and so she dreamed of the white sails and wondered if some day she would be like them and drift out beyond the horizon...seeking...finding....

Trina grew to womanhood in the turbulent times around 1864 when the Germans were massing their troops behind the great wall of Dannevirke, the southern border of their beloved Denmark. She met Peder Bursen, a young man from across the channel, who had been forced into the German army after the fall of Dannevirke. He finally secured his release from the army, but he knew he could be recalled at any time. Having married Trina, and not wishing to go back to serve the Germans again, he talked her parents and others into going with him and Trina to America.

Letters from relatives who had already gone to the United States attracted many Scandinavians to follow. In 1886, Peter Nielsen, living in Missouri, wrote to his brother Wilhelm back in Denmark.

You write that you are having a bad time at home, as I can well imagine, and I doubt that it will get much better. If I can find a good place for you over here, will you come over? And if so, send me your answer immediately. I think I can get you a job with the same man I work for. You can earn six kroner a day. You can save an average of 80 kroner a month, and you will live well.... If you decide to come, you can just write to me and let me know when you will leave home and by which steamship line you will travel. Just think of such a journey as though it is a journey to Copenhagen, except that it takes somewhat longer, and if you come and don't like it here, you can go home again; but I assure you that you will like America; it is a free country and a money country. You need never lack anything, as long as you are a bachelor.

Immigrants sometimes returned to their native country for visits, and their obvious prosperity increased interest in immigration. Sofus Neble (the man dressed in white), a Danish American newspaper editor, returned to Copenhagen around 1920. The car, a status symbol that only a few could afford, demonstrated his success in America.

Axel Jarlson remembered the reasons why so many members of his family of eight brothers and sisters left for the United States at the end of the 19th century.

My uncle Olaf used to come to us between voyages, and he was all the time talking about America; what a fine place it was to make money in. He said that he would long ago have settled down on shore there, but that he had a mate's place on a ship and hoped some day to be captain. In America they gave you good land for nothing, and in two years you could be a rich man; and no one had to go in the army unless he wanted to. That was what my uncle told us.

There was a school house to which I and two of my sisters went all the winter—for education is compulsory in Sweden—and the schoolmaster told us one day about the great things that poor Swedes had done in America. They grew rich and powerful like noblemen and they even held Government offices. It was true, also, that no one had to go in the army unless he wanted to be a soldier. With us all the young men who are strong have to go in the army, because Sweden expects to have to fight Russia some day. The army takes the young men away from their work and makes hard times in the family.

A man who had been living in America once came to visit the little village that was near our cottage. He wore gold rings set with jewels and had a fine watch. He said that food was cheap in America and that a man could earn nearly ten times as much there as in Sweden. He treated all the men to brandvin, or brandy wine, as some call it, and there seemed to be no end to his money.

Albertina Asukas with her children in Pantane, Uuro, Finland, around 1898. At this time her husband, Samuel, was working in America. The oldest son, Johan Jacob (standing in back), immigrated to Worcester, Massachusetts, in 1912.

It was after this that father and mother were both sick during all of one winter, and we had nothing to eat, except black bread and a sort of potato soup or gruel, with now and then a herring. We had to sell our cows and we missed the milk and cheese.

So at last it was decided that my brother was to go to America, and we spent the last day bidding him good-bye, as if we should never see him again. My mother and sisters cried a great deal, and begged him to write; my father told him not to forget us in that far off country, but to do right and all would be well, and my uncle said that he would become a leader of the people....

We got a letter every month from my brother. He kept doing better and better, and at last he wrote that a farm had been given to him by the Government. It was sixty acres of land, good soil, with plenty of timber on it and a river running alongside. He had two fine horses and a wagon and sleigh, and he was busy clearing the land. He wanted his brother, Eric, to go to him, but we could not spare Eric, and so Knut, the third brother, was sent. He helped Gustaf for two years, and then he took a sixty-acre farm. Both sent money home to us, and soon they sent tickets for Hilda and Christine, two of my sisters.

The names of American cities were almost magical to Scandinavian children. Didrik Arup Seip, born in 1884, grew up in a remote town in southern Norway. He recalled hearing about the United States.

When I was a boy, I learned the name of America before I heard of any other country. I heard about New York and Chicago before London and Berlin. Names like Dakota and Minnesota were better known to me than Spain and France. This was due to the fact that I grew up in a mountain community which had sent many of its young men and even some of its women to America. Letters as well as Norwegian-American newspapers came all the time. Far up in that mountain valley we were in lively cultural contact with America, receiving reports that gave life a wider horizon and nourished our imaginations.

Hilma Salvon was born in Finland in 1895 and came to the United States with her family when she was 11. She grew up during a period when the Russian Empire was attempting to exert greater control over its Finnish subjects.

Finland was under Russian rule then. Russia demanded soldiers from Finland and they were protesting against it, the whole Finland. They were going around with these lists, everybody to sign. There was a general strike. Everything was in confusion and everything was standing still. Father and many Finns, if they could, just flew to America. He wrote to his cousin here in Astoria [Oregon] that he'd like to come to America and he sends a ticket from America—well, you go. My father came in 1905. We were left in Finland, because Mother was expecting. Then that baby was born in January and then we left in 1906.

Walter Lindstrom came to the United States from Sweden in 1913. He remembered how reading books by American authors led him to decide to emigrate.

The library at our public school was a treasure house, full of books from the whole world. It had *Robinson Crusoe, Gulliver's Travels, Uncle Tom's Cabin, Huckleberry Finn*, Jack London, *Tom Sawyer, Around the World in Eighty Days*. There was no end to what we could choose from. Nor was this all. The boys in the neighborhood and I ganged up and bought paperbound books every week from a bookstore in the city on the mainland; books the school library didn't have—Sherlock Holmes, Nick Carter, Buffalo Bill. We never bothered to look at the names of the authors. It was what was inside the covers that interested us. Buffalo Bill, for instance. What a man! And what a country. America! Huckleberry Finn, Tom Sawyer, running away from conformity on a raft in the river to freedom, where they didn't have to comb their hair or take orders from the widow. You could probably say that it was because of those books that I finally came to America.

Rodolph Holmberg, a second-generation Finnish American, described why his parents left Finland at the turn of the century.

Like most immigrants of that period, they heard the fabulous stories going through Finland, and I presume through all the European countries of the opportunities in this new world that the inhabitants of those countries didn't have.

To give you an example, my father spent his childhood traveling around Finland by foot. His mother was a harness maker. They would go from peasant home to peasant home, and would repair the harnesses—the leather. When the work was completed they would bed and board there, and then they would move on to the next home.

Although my father had this opportunity to travel through Finland, he never had the opportunity to obtain any formal education. Being uneducated, he felt the kind of job he would get in Finland would keep him poor. To avoid this kind of life he came over here in search of work.

Hannah Sippala, born in Finland in 1897, came to the United States in 1916. She remembered that she, too, caught "America fever."

I want to come [to] America. I get the America fever, they said. And when I heard some people go to America, I said, "I want to go too." But my father and mother don't like me to go. And I said, "I lay down on the bed and you can feed me here if you don't let me go to America." And father said, "We don't want to feed grown people there. Let her go." My mother said she'd let me die before she'd let me go [to] America!

Then they give me money; and they give enough money, if I change my mind, I can come back. First, I told them I'm happy because I want to come. But when I got over, I almost came back. But I'm so ashamed to go back, because I want to come so bad.

As an old woman, Jennie Monson of Chicago wrote a letter to a researcher in Sweden, explaining why she left Småland in 1904. Her family lived on a croft, or tenant farm, that was part of a large manor.

For us...it can be said in two words. Poverty and inferiority. We could never dress like others and we were almost afraid to look at people. As soon as I was big enough, there was hard work, and I had to go to the manor every day from six in the morning to seven-thirty in the evening. The lease for the little croft was paid for with three men's workdays and three women's or children's workdays a week.

State governments in the United States, eager to populate their territory, advertised overseas for settlers. South Dakota printed this pamphlet in Norwegian to attract immigrants.

Syd Dakota

Verdens rigeste Kornkammer.

Et Land fuldt af Solskin

Sundt Klima   Lykkelige Mennesker

Dets frugtbare Marker, blomstrende Stæder og voksende Industri indbyder Dem og byder Dem gylden Anledning til Livsophold

Udgivet af
STATENS INDVANDRINGSBUREAU

Chas. McCaffree, Kommissær
Pierre, S. Dak.

Hilma Swenson Anderson (right) with her brother and a friend prepare to sail for the United States in 1910. It was the custom in Sweden to present emigrants with flowers when they left.

CHAPTER TWO

COMING TO THE UNITED STATES

A few Scandinavians came to what is now the United States during colonial times. Henrich Christiansen, a Danish ship captain, sailed up the Hudson River in the early 1600s, trading with Native Americans.

There were many Danish settlers in the Dutch colony of New Netherlands. Jonas Bronck, a Dane who arrived in 1629, purchased a large tract of land from Native Americans. Called Bronck's farm, it is today the Bronx, the northernmost borough of New York City. Jochem Pietersen Keyter, Bronck's brother-in-law, was the first European settler in what is now the neighborhood of Harlem on Manhattan Island.

Sweden established a colony in North America in 1638. The settlers—about one-third of whom were Finns—arrived on the banks of the Delaware River in a ship named *Kalmar Nyckel* (The Key of Kalmar). They built a settlement called Christina, named after Sweden's queen, a 12-year-old girl. Today, the site is part of Wilmington, Delaware.

The Swedes and Finns constructed the first log cabins in the New World. By cutting notches at the ends of felled trees, the settlers could stack them to form cabin walls without using nails. Countless other pioneers throughout the United States would later build such cabins as their homes. However, the Swedish colony was short-lived. A few years after its founding, the Dutch captured it.

The early Swedish and Finnish settlers remained. In the next 150 years, a few other Scandinavians followed. Most of them were sailors who jumped ship to start a new life in the American colonies.

It was an American of Swedish or Finnish background, John Morton (born Mortonson), who cast the deciding vote when the Continental Congress declared American independence in 1776. Swedish Americans also like to claim that one of their own, John Hanson, was the first president of the United States. Actually, Hanson was elected president of the Congress of the Confederation, the first governing body of the new United States, in 1781. (George Washington did not take office until 1789.)

Norwegians formed the first large, organized group of Scandinavians to emigrate to the United States in the 19th century. About 80 percent of Norway's population lived in rural areas. Most of them resented the city-dwellers who formed the business and governmental elite and the clergy of the nation. A religious movement that opposed the state-sponsored Lutheran Church won many followers among Norway's farmers.

Cleng Peerson, one of these religious dissenters, led the first group of Norwegian immigrants to the United States. Peerson traveled alone to America in 1821 to find land for a communal farm in northern New York State. Four years later, 52 people, mostly married couples and children, sailed from the port of Stavanger on a small sailing ship named *Restauration* (Restoration). The journey to the United States took them 14 weeks.

After meeting Peerson in New York City, the immigrants traveled up the Hudson River and through the new Erie Canal to what became known as the Kendall Settlement, named for a township in northern New York.

Conditions there were not as favorable as Peerson had hoped. He began to look farther west, traveling on foot to Illinois. In 1835, he led some of the Kendall settlers and new immigrants to the Fox River Valley, near today's Ottawa, Illinois.

Peerson, a restless person, wandered on to join other Norwegian settlements in Missouri, Iowa, and Texas. There he found other Norwegian immigrants like himself— rebels who opposed the stifling social conditions in Norway and who had sought freedom in the United States.

The early Norwegian settlers began to write letters to relatives and friends back home. Such "America letters" were read aloud in villages and reprinted in newspapers. In the late 1830s, popular handbooks for emigrants began to appear.

One of these, *True Account of America*, by Ole Rynning, gave the following advice: "The best time to leave Norway is so early in the spring as to be able to reach the place of settlement by midsummer.... In that way something can be raised even the first year."

Leaders of Norway's Lutheran Church tried to discourage the departure of so many of its younger members. In 1837, Bishop John Neumann warned his flock: "Here in Norway rest the ashes of your forefathers.... Here you are still surrounded by relatives and friends who share your joy and your sorrow, while there [in America], when you are far away from all that has been dear to you, who shall close your eyes in the last hour of life? A stranger's hand! And who shall weep at your grave? Perhaps—no one!"

But for Norwegians, the great appeal of the United States was its social equality. In the United States, as one letter-writer reported, "Here it is not asked what or who was your father, but the question is, what are you?"

Norwegians responded eagerly to such prospects. Their homeland had been dominated for four centuries by Denmark, and was now under Sweden's thumb. In 1820, the population of Norway was about 1,000,000. Between then and 1925, approximately 800,000 Norwegians immigrated to the United

States. Norway saw a greater proportion of its people leave for the United States than any other nation except Ireland.

New immigrants from Sweden started to arrive in the 1840s and 1850s. Most came as family groups. The earliest ones boarded cargo ships that carried Swedish iron ore to America. One of the most influential was Gustaf Unonius, a graduate of the University of Uppsala. With his wife and several friends, Unonius came to the United States in 1841. They founded a colony named New Uppsala about 30 miles west of Mil-

A young Norwegian woman loads the wagon that will take her on the first leg of her journey to America around 1900.

waukee, Wisconsin. Unonius's letters to a Swedish newspaper, reporting that both land and work were available, attracted others. (Unonius himself returned to Sweden in 1859, disappointed at his failure to make a living in America.)

Swedish emigrant societies were formed in the 1840s. They published booklets that gave prospective immigrants advice such as what they should take on the voyage or how to acquire land in the United States.

After about 1865, mass immigration from Sweden began. At this time, Sweden was suffering from overpopulation, and famine struck the rural areas. Between 1868 and 1873 about 100,000 Swedes left for the United States. The majority were unmarried men in search of jobs.

Many more headed across the Atlantic in the 1880s; more than 90,000 Swedish immigrants arrived in 1888 alone. Most of them were farmers whose crops could not compete with low-priced imported wheat from the United States and the Ukraine. Others were miners and loggers from northern Sweden who also suffered from foreign competition.

The establishment of Swedish communities in the United States created a magnet for other newcomers. In 1891, the Swedish Aid Society of New York was formed to help newcomers find jobs. Soon, many unmarried women felt secure enough to make the journey by themselves. After about 1890, in fact, more Swedish women than men immigrated to the United States.

Between 1851 and 1930, about 2.1 million Swedes came to the United States—in absolute numbers, more than from any other Scandinavian country. The entire population of Sweden was only about 5 million in 1900.

Danes also started to emigrate in large numbers in the 1840s. The first Danish emigrant guidebooks appeared in 1847. Rasmus Sørensen, a member of the Danish parliament, published a series of pamphlets about the United States based on letters from his son in Wisconsin. Sørensen himself emigrated to Wisconsin with the rest of his family in 1852.

Religion played a role in some Danes' decision to emigrate. In 1847, American members of the Church of Jesus Christ of Latter-day Saints, or Mormons, established a base in what is now the state of Utah. A former Danish sailor was among them. At his urging, the Mormons sent missionaries to Denmark in 1850. Over the next few decades, more than 12,000 Danish converts left their homeland to settle in Utah.

In 1864, Denmark lost about one-fourth of its territory in a war with Prussia. Many Danes in the conquered lands also emigrated to the United States. By this time, Denmark had more people than the relatively small nation could provide jobs for. Farm laborers who could not find work at home made up more than 40 percent of Danish immigrants in the last three decades of the 19th century. Most of the rest were unskilled laborers and craftspeople.

Mogens Abraham Sommer, a harsh critic of the Danish government, founded an emigration agency in Copenhagen in the 1860s. He personally led many groups across the Atlantic.

Though families often emigrated together until the 1870s, after that time the majority of Danish immigrants were single. About 60 percent of them were men. After they began to prosper, some of these men proposed to sweethearts they had left in Denmark, sending them ship tickets if they accepted the offer of marriage. About one-fourth of the migrants paid for their ship tickets with money orders sent from friends or relatives in the United States.

The majority of Danes left home from the German ports of Hamburg or Bremen, where large steamship companies were located. In 1879, the Danish Thingvalla Line began direct service from Copenhagen to New York City. By steamship, the trip lasted between one and two weeks.

Danish immigration continued at a relatively high level until 1924. The peak year was 1882, when more than 11,000 Danes arrived. Between 1850 and 1900, about 245,000 Danes emigrated to the United States—one-tenth of Denmark's

A group of hopeful Danish immigrants waits to board the ship that will take them to the United States in 1923.

total population in 1900. Since then, approximately 100,000 more emigrants have arrived from Denmark.

In the 1830s and 1840s, when both Finland and Alaska were under the control of the Russian Empire, a small number of Finns went to work in Alaska. One of them, Arvid A. Etholén, became governor of the territory.

Beginning in 1864, Finns living in northern Norway began to go to Michigan to work in the mines.

Their letters back home gradually drew more immigrants, some from Finland itself. As in Sweden and Denmark, the rural areas of Finland suffered from overpopulation and dwindling economic opportunities. As one Finnish immigrant recalled, "I came to get a little butter on top of the bread."

Between 1870 and 1920, about 300,000 Finns arrived in the United States. The majority (75 percent between 1901 and 1920) were young unmarried adults between 16 and 30 years old.

Finnish emigrants usually made their way to English ports on the North Sea. From there they took trains to Liverpool, the main departure point for transatlantic ships. Some Finns also left Europe from the north German port of Bremerhaven.

Icelanders retained their separate identity and language during five centuries of rule by Norway and Denmark. Modern Icelandic is almost the same as the language of the ancient *Eddas*.

A few Icelanders, converts to the Mormon religion, settled in Utah around 1855. Ten years later William Wickmann, a Dane who had worked in Iceland, emigrated to Milwaukee. He wrote enthusiastic letters to his Icelandic friends. These were passed from hand to hand, setting off a wave of emigration.

An Icelandic settlement was founded in 1870 on Washington Island in Lake Michigan, at the entrance to Green Bay. Between 1870 and 1900, about 15,000 Icelanders arrived in the United States—about one-fifth of Iceland's total population. Most settled in North Dakota. But since 1918, when Iceland won virtual independence, very few citizens have left home.

LEAVING HOME

Leaving home required careful preparations. D. A. Peterson moved to Iowa from Sweden with his family in 1849. Years later, he remembered the days before the journey.

We were harassed daily by our neighbors who came to see the preparation for our leave-taking, and who were always proffering advice, and many of them sadly bewailing the fate in store for us, such as falling into the hands of the Turks (the terror of them have not yet died out in the lower classes in Europe), shipwrecks, famine, all these painted in most vivid colors. Many, though, wished themselves ready to start on the journey; with most of them means to carry out the wish was lacking.

Many Scandinavians traveled to Liverpool, England, to take an ocean liner to the United States. Johannes Swenson, the nephew of S. M. Swenson, the first Swede to settle in Texas, described his experiences in Liverpool.

When we approached Liverpool the entire stretch was that of a huge factory town—high chimneys and from all dense smoke columns rose to the sky.
Finally we arrived in Liverpool and after leaving the train, the three baggage cars were switched to another track and we were hustled off to an emigrant hotel with Mr. Lyon and Mr. Heard at the head, a policeman on either side, and one in the rear so that no one would get lost. The emigrant agent who met us was a half-blood Negro. There was a frightful commotion when our luggage was to be transferred from the railway to the *S.S. City of Baltimore* as a carload had disappeared and could not be located. What should we do? All our possessions were in these freight cars and no one would leave Liverpool without his belongings. We were compelled to go aboard the *City of Baltimore* and Mr. Lyon assured us that our effects would be located and shipped to New York. However, just as the Atlantic steamer was lifting its anchor we saw a small boat approach our steamer at high speed. All eyes were fixed on the little boat and as it came closer we recognized Mr. Lyon in the bow waving with an object in his hand. In a few minutes it was alongside and soon everything was on board and the *City of Baltimore* was gliding out of Liverpool harbor on the afternoon of June 20 with about one thousand passengers and a crew of one hundred twenty-five.

Saying good-bye to family and friends was, for many, the most difficult part of the journey. These Swedes left the Dalarna region in 1899.

A family leaves its village in 1906. In the isolated mountains and valleys of Norway, boats as well as carts and trains were necessary to get to the ports of departure.

Marie Jørgensen left Denmark in 1895 with her six children to join her husband who had emigrated to Michigan three years earlier. She booked passage on the Danish Thingvalla Line, which left from Copenhagen. But before the ship reached the Atlantic, she had to make a heartbreaking decision.

The day before we reached Kristiansand [Norway], Oscar [a son] complained about his throat. I put more clothes on him, and he lay down in the afternoon, and the day we reached Kristiansand he seemed better. He was up on deck in the sunshine and ate well; but I did ask to speak with the doctor in the morning to get something for the pain in his throat, but the doctor had gone ashore. I did not see him until the ship was ready to sail. He examined the boy, and his words were like the voice of doom to me, and I shall never forget them as long as I live: "The boy has diphtheria; he must go ashore in Kristiansand"!—I cried and begged for him to be left on board, but in vain; I had to go ashore with the other children, but I could not have our baggage, and I could not under any circumstances see the boy while he was ill. Then they sent for the head doctor at the hospital. He, too, said it was diphtheria, but comforted me and said: "We have things to treat it with, Madam." Then we went ashore and telephoned for a man from the hospital to come and get the boy. How unhappy he was, the poor boy, he cried and begged, "Let me stay on the ship; they cannot tell me what to do, only you can do that"! I told him about Søren's Jens who went to the hospital last spring and was cured. I explained to him that if he stayed on the ship he would die and be put into the Atlantic Ocean. Finally, he calmed down because I promised that we would wait for him. He would only be taken ashore to have his throat swabbed. Then he went with the man and nodded up to me. I followed him with my eyes for as long as I could, and then I cried—yes, I cried as I sailed from Norway as I had not cried when we left Denmark. Yes, it is terrible to be separated from a child so brutally and to have to send him away from me with a lie! "I do not want to go to bed there," he kept saying.— I pray to God that the bed there will not be his last. The doctor on

An "America chest"— like this Norwegian one from around 1916— carried items the immigrant believed were necessary for a new life in the United States. This trunk contained scissors, a cup, and a Bible, along with clothes and linens. The "America chest" also displayed examples of Old Country artistry, such as skillful embroidery.

Immigrant Songs

The immigrants from Scandinavia often composed songs on the journey. Here is a sampling.

Brothers, we have far to go,
Across the salty water,
And then there is America,
Upon the other shore.
Surely it's not possible?
Oh yes, it's so delightful!
Pity that America,
Pity that America
Must lie so far away.
　　　—*Swedish song*

Farewell, valley that I cherish,
Farewell, church and trees and home,
Farewell parson, farewell parish
Farewell kith and kin, my own,
Lovely gardens, walks of beauty,—
Would to God this were undone!—
Home, you stay me in my duty,
Calling, "Leave me not, my son!"
　　　—*Norwegian song*

I'll embark from Hankoniemi
On a small boat and go
'Cause Finland can't feed
The children of the poor.
　　　—*Finnish song*

board said that the illness would last about 10 days. A letter was written to the Thingvalla agent in Kristiansand, asking him to send the boy with the next Thingvalla ship. [Oscar joined his family in Michigan a month after Marie and the other children arrived.]

Irja Laaksonen immigrated to the United States in 1907 with her mother and siblings to join her father, who had left the year before. In her journal, Laaksonen described the trip.

Turku, Finland. December, 1907. Except for the jingle of sleigh bells and the muffled thud of the horses' hoofs on the snowy street, the night was silent and dark as pitch. The stars in the Milky Way seemed to blink their good-byes to us.

"Mama," I cried, "the stars are following us! Are they going to America, too?" Mama said yes the stars would be there too.

We were on our way to stay overnight at Grandpa's house. The next day Grandpa and our six cousins would wave good-bye to us as we boarded the train for the Finnish seaport of Hanko. There we would find the ship that would take us across the Baltic and North seas to England.

I don't recall boarding the ship—I was only four years old at the time. I do remember seeing many people sitting around on the crowded deck. There were families with lots of children. Bundles and suitcases were piled everywhere.

The journey across the North Sea was rough. We were all laid low with seasickness, except for my brother Ilmari. He was only six and one-half years old, but such a little man! He waited on all of us, bringing us tea and oranges. We had never tasted these exotic foods before, and we marveled at their strong, wonderful aroma. To this day the smell of oranges brings back memories of that ocean trip.

We landed at Hull, England, and boarded a streetcar to take us to what Mama called the "Immigrant's Hotel." I remember that I was the last of my family to scramble onto the crowded car. Panic swept over me at the thought that it would leave without me. The buildings looked big and gray—in fact, everything looked gray. Even the cobblestones in the street appeared very big and gray.

The next day we took a train across England to Liverpool where we boarded the White Star Liner, *Arabic*.

Henny Hale recalled the excitement of her journey from Norway in 1923. Her uncle in Tacoma, Washington, had sent a ship ticket.

I got the ticket, and like I say, I had hardly been off the farm. I didn't know what the world was all about. But I had to take the boat and go into the nearest city...to get my papers in order. That's the first time I saw an electric light. No kidding. I didn't know what I let myself in for, but I wanted to go to America, *period*; so I went to get these papers in order and I made it....

What I remember more than anything was my little brother going with me down to where we took the boat to row across; and he stood there with his fists like this and stuck them in his pocket and he wasn't going to cry. My dad went with me; he

The Finnish passengers of the Gripsholm, *bound for America, in front of the Northern Museum in Stockholm. This group of 281 travelers managed to get in some sight-seeing before sailing on the Swedish America Line in 1929.*

rowed me across that sea there. Then there was a small place, maybe four or five blocks long, to walk from the boat and over to the ship that I was going on. My dad helped me with my suitcase and he walked half of the way with me. And I turned around and I kissed him before I left—the only time in my life I kissed my father. I never did kiss my mother. Because you didn't have emotions; you weren't supposed to. He turned around and walked home again. He was really glad that I could get out of there....

We sailed from Eidet down the coast and we stopped in Bodø where my sister worked at that time, so she came to the boat and gave me a blanket. In Bergen, we took the train to Oslo. I was alone till I came on the train; then we met people that was going to America and we got to talking. In Oslo, we had to stay overnight and we went out for a tour of Karl Johan [the main street] and it was fun. I thought I had an awful lot of money so I went into a *butikk* [store] and I bought myself a green hat and I paid thirty crowns for it. Oh, gee, I paid thirty crowns for a green hat, a green silk hat. I remember that green silk hat all my life. And I came to Tacoma with, I think, forty-two cents.

Jacob Riis, who would later become a famous photojournalist, recalled the gift his friends in Ribe, Denmark, gave him when he left for the United States.

So I went out in the world to seek my fortune, the richer for some $40 which Ribe friends had presented to me, knowing that I had barely enough to pay my passage over in the steerage. Though I had aggravated them in a hundred ways and wholly disturbed the peace of the old town, I think they liked me a little, anyway. They were always good, kind neighbors, honest and lovable folk. I looked back with my mother's blessing yet in my ears, to where the gilt weather-vanes glistened on her father's house, and the tears brimmed over again. And yet, such is life, presently I felt my heart bound with new courage. All was not lost yet. The world was before me.

The emigration office in Århus, Denmark, was on this street. In 1909, when this picture was taken, many Danes went there for information and tickets to America.

CROSSING THE OCEAN

Torben Lange, a middle-class Dane from a town northwest of Copenhagen, sailed to the United States in 1846. He traveled as a steerage passenger on the Washington, *which left from Cuxhaven, Germany. Lange described the journey in a letter home.*

The most unpleasant thing about the voyage were the villanous passengers. You would have to search long and hard to find such a blasphemous brood of vipers. I've never seen a gang like them. With the exception of four or five families...they were all rejects—foul language and cheating all day long.... Most of them were well educated.

Steerage became a regular brothel. People gambled their clothes away and fistfights ensued. We had four prostitutes and at least five thieves. One of the latter was searched, and it was discovered that he had stolen thirty-one different items, including one of my handkerchiefs. One thief stole from the next. One of them wanted to jump overboard but was held back. When finally released he decided not to jump.

A large sausage, two glasses, and the old knife and fork I received from Grethe were stolen from me. I got the fork back again. I told the thief, who came from Holstein, that I knew he had stolen it. I said that if he gave it back I would keep my mouth shut, but if not I would report him to the police in New York.

In 1888, as a young man of 17, Birger Osland came to the United States from Stavanger, Norway.

We traveled third class or steerage, and were well satisfied with our lot. There were people of many nationalities on the steamer—English, Scotch, Scandinavians, Germans, and some Poles and Russians. One day we had a concert in which members of each nationality displayed their talents. Andreas Rygg and I represented the Scandinavian

The trip on sailing ships in the first half of the 1800s could take months. Still, when the weather was fair, passengers amused themselves by dancing.

element, and we chose to sing a Swedish song in first and second tenor, to the apparent delight of our audience.

Our appetites were excellent during the voyage and the food was good. At mealtimes we all lined up in front of the cook's galley, holding our tin pails, into which the cook ladled generous helpings of good Scottish soup. In the deep-flanged lids, turned up, he put meat, potatoes, and bread. Just once during our ten- or eleven-day crossing did we have a real storm. The hatches were battened down tight, and there were no passengers on deck except my two friends and myself and a Norwegian sea captain who shared our four-berth cabin. None of us three boys had eaten much that noon and we expected to be able to weather the storm in as good trim as the old sea captain. Suddenly I felt an irresistible impulse in my stomach, and to hide my shame I rushed down to our cabin, grabbed a pail which I thought was mine, and surrendered to the urge. In my misery I did not notice that the old sea captain had followed me. He probably intended to be of help, but I soon felt his firm fingers around my neck and heard his angry voice, "What in hell are you doing in my pail?"

On board the Hellig Olav *(Saint Olaf) in 1904, Norwegian passengers gather on deck during the trip to America.*

Maren Lorensen received a pre-paid ticket from her brother and journeyed to Racine, Wisconsin, from Denmark in 1893. She wrote to a friend back home describing her trip.

It was really cold when I left. We nearly froze to death up on deck, but it would have been dreadful to stay down in the cabin the whole time. There was such a smell of vomit as we were all seasick. For my part, I was sick for almost the whole trip; but we had strong winds, and then, of course, it is worst, and we were treated like dogs on the ship as it was an English ship I was on, and they are not so nice as the Danish ones. But I had to travel with the English as brother Søren sent me a ticket for that line. We had our food just like the pigs in Denmark, and I doubt they would have eaten it.... When the ship rolled from one side to the other, we and everything that was loose on the ship tumbled back and forth all mixed together, and most threw up and slid back and forth in that. Yes, I shudder at the thought; I would not make that trip again for anything. When we finally got to America, all our clothes were fumigated to disinfect them, yes what a lot of fuss that was.

Hans Fahl, who came to the United States from Sweden in 1923, described his voyage to an interviewer.

I came on the motorship *Stockholm* and there was one incident on that trip which I'll never forget. It happened to be the anniversary of the sinking of *Titanic*. And we came to the very spot where this *Titanic* sank and the ship stops there for twenty minutes. And they had a beautiful memorial service for those 1,500 people that disappeared in the water, and then they threw a big wreath of flowers down in the ocean. It was, I think, the eleventh anniversary of the sinking of *Titanic*. A day or so before, why somebody said, "There's an iceberg over there!"

In the 20th century, steamships made the ocean trip shorter and more comfortable. These Danish passengers were photographed in 1930.

Swedish folk dancers perform in Fort Christina Park in Wilmington, Delaware. In the background is the statue designed by Swedish American sculptor Carl Milles in 1938 to commemorate the 300th anniversary of the founding of the Swedish colony. At the top of the monument is a representation of the Kalmar Nyckel, *the ship that carried the original colonists.*

SCANDINAVIANS IN COLONIAL AMERICA

Johan Printz, the governor of New Sweden, described the colony in 1653, only two years before it was conquered by the Dutch. Later that year, Printz returned to Sweden.

The people yet living and remaining in New Sweden, men, women, and children, number altogether two hundred souls. The settled families do well, and are supplied with cattle. The country yields a fair revenue. Still the soldiers and others in the Company's service enjoy but a very mean subsistence, and consequently seek opportunity every day to get away, whether with or without leave, having no expectation of any release, as it is now five and a half years since a letter was received from home. The English trade, from which we used to obtain good support, is at an end, on account of the war with Holland; while the fur trade yields no profit, particularly now that hostilities have broken out between the Arrihoga and the Susquehanna Indians, from whom the beavers were procured.

On May 31, 1693, Charles Christopher Springer, a member of the Swedish church at Fort Christina, wrote to the postmaster in Gothenburg, Sweden. The former Swedish colony was by now part of the English colonies. The letter, signed by 30 other Swedish residents, asked that two ministers be sent to "instruct our youth." It was the first of the "America letters."

As to what concerns our situation in this country, we are for the most part husbandmen. We plough and sow and till the ground; and as to our meat and drink, we live according to the old Swedish customs. This country is very rich and fruitful, and here grow all sorts of grain in great plenty, so that we are richly supplied with meat and drink; and we send out yearly to our neighbors on this continent and the neighboring islands, bread, grain, flour, and oil. We have here also all sorts of beasts, fowls and fishes. Our wives and daughters employ themselves in spinning wool and flax, and many of them in weaving; so we have great reason to thank the Almighty for his manifold mercies and benefits. God grant that we may also have good shepherds to feed us with his Holy Word and sacraments. We likewise live in peace and friendship with one another; and the Indians have not molested us for many years.

Further, since this country has ceased to be under the government of Sweden, we are bound to acknowledge and declare, for the sake of truth, that we have been well and kindly treated, as well by the Dutch, as by His Majesty, the King of England, our gracious sovereign; on the other hand, we, the

Swedes, have been and still are, true and faithful to him in words and deeds. We have always had at our head good and gracious magistrates; and we live with one another in peace and amity.

Four years after Springer sent his letter, two Swedish clergymen, Andrew Rudman and Eric Biörk, arrived in the colony with religious literature. Biörk wrote a letter to Sweden from Christina Creek in October 1697.

The country here is delightful, as it has always been described, and overflows with every blessing; so that the people live very well without being compelled to too much or too severe labor. The taxes are very light; the farmers, after their work is over, live as they do in Sweden, but are clothed as well as the respectable inhabitants of the towns. They have fresh meat and fish in abundance, and want nothing of what other countries produce; they have plenty of grain wherewith to make bread, and plenty of drink. May God continue them in the enjoyment of these blessings. There are no poor in this country, but they all provide for themselves, for the land is rich and fruitful, and no man who will labor can suffer want.

The Indians and we are as one people; we live in much greater friendship with them than with the English; they call the Swedes in their language their own people; they were very glad when we came, as they see now that Sweden does not abandon them. They are also very fond of learning the catechism, which has been printed in their language; they like to have it read to them, and they have engaged Mr. Charles Springer to teach their children to read it.

Peter Kalm, a student of the Swedish biologist Karl Linneas, visited the English colonies in 1750. He entered some observations into his journal on May 7.

In the morning we continued our journey from near Maurice River down to Cape May. We had a Swedish guide along who was probably born of Swedish parents, and was married to a Swedish woman but who could not, himself, speak Swedish. There are many such here of both sexes; for since English is the principal language in the land all people gradually get to speak that, and they become ashamed to talk in their own tongue, because they fear they may not in such a case be real English. Consequently many Swedish women are married to English men, and although they can speak Swedish very well it is impossible to make them do so, and when they are spoken to in Swedish they always answer in English. The same condition obtains among the men; so that it is easy to see that the Swedish language is doomed to extinction in America; and in fifty or sixty years' time there will not be many left who can understand Swedish, and still less of those who can converse in it.

John Morton

In the summer of 1776, delegates from the 13 American colonies gathered at the Continental Congress in Philadelphia. They debated whether to declare independence from Great Britain, and they agreed that the resolution for independence must have the support of all 13 delegations. On July 1, 9 delegations voted in favor of the resolution.

Pennsylvania was among the colonies that failed to support independence that day. Two of its five delegates were in favor, and two opposed. The fifth delegate, John Morton, was undecided. Morton's friend, Benjamin Franklin, asked him to vote in favor of independence. If Pennsylvania supported independence, Franklin argued, the remaining delegations would follow its lead.

On July 2, 1776, John Morton cast his vote: "Aye." Two days later, he and 51 others signed the Declaration of Independence. But without Morton's vote, the resolution might have failed.

Morton was a descendant of the settlers of the Swedish colony in Delaware. His great-grandfather, Morton Mortonson, came from Finland (then part of Sweden) in 1654. Mortonson built a log cabin near Philadelphia that is still standing. It is possible that John Morton was born in it around 1724.

John Morton devoted himself to public life. He served as a judge, sheriff, and member of the Pennsylvania Assembly. The burning issue of his time was the colonies' stormy relationship with England. In 1765 Morton served as a delegate to the Stamp Act Congress, which protested the British tax on printed matter such as newspapers, pamphlets, and legal documents.

The step from launching protests to demanding independence was a difficult one, however. Morton was known as a moderate. He worked hard to heal the breach between the colonists and England. His support for independence cost him the friendship of many of his neighbors. They called him a traitor. Morton's relatives believed that this hastened his death, which occurred the next year.

But Morton remained proud of his vote. On his deathbed, he stated: "Tell them that they will live to see the hour when they shall acknowledge that my vote for independence has been the most glorious service that I ever rendered to my country."

On arrival, a family gazes out into New York Harbor. A new life lies ahead.

CHAPTER THREE

THE NEW LAND

ustaf Unonius, who arrived in the United States in 1841, wrote, "We were surprised to find that in New York most people knew less about Illinois or Iowa than we did." The newcomers, by contrast, had already read immigrant guidebooks that informed them that land in the Midwest was both cheap and fertile.

Those who landed at New York City usually continued their journey. Often, they went by boat up the Hudson River, through the Erie Canal, and into the Great Lakes. From there, they could travel to the midwestern states.

Some Scandinavians landed in New Orleans and went up the Mississippi River. Others ended their sea voyage in Canada and traveled overland to Michigan, Wisconsin, Illinois, Minnesota, and other states.

In 1855, New York State opened a landing station for immigrants at Castle Garden, off the southern tip of Manhattan Island. Castle Garden had earlier been a theater. It held a special significance for Scandinavians. In 1850, Jenny Lind—"the Swedish nightingale" who was perhaps the most renowned singer of the 19th century—had given a concert there on her tour of the United States. Some Scandinavian immigrants believed (incorrectly) that she had bought the island as a refuge for immigrants.

Jon Halldorsson, an Icelandic immigrant, described his stay at Castle Garden in 1872: "[We] found ourselves in a huge building, accommodating thousands of people. We spent the night there. We had to buy our food, but room on the floor and on benches in the building was free."

Castle Garden was intended to protect the immigrants against swindlers who tried to fleece them of their money. The newcomers could buy railroad or boat tickets there, exchange their foreign money at honest rates, and obtain information about lodging and employment opportunities.

As the tide of immigration swelled, the United States government became concerned. In 1892, it established an immigration station at Ellis Island in New York Harbor. Here immigrants were inspected for diseases and questioned about their ability to support themselves. After 1909, each immigrant was supposed to have $25 so that he or she would not "become a public charge"—that is, depend on charity.

As Charles T. Anderson, a Swede who arrived in 1925, recalled, it was possible to evade the rule. "Twenty-five dollars? I didn't have it. I told [the inspector] I had it but I didn't have it. I spent it already. I didn't have a red cent in my pocket when I landed on that boat. They didn't check. He just said something like, 'Have you got $25?' So I just said yes, and that's it. I had nothing. That's something I put over on them."

It was harder, however, to bypass the line of doctors who examined immigrants for a variety of ailments. Some immigrants were turned away and had to return to their native lands. Others were held at Ellis Island until their cases could be judged.

Annette Andersen recalled the words of her Danish mother, who went through Ellis Island in 1916. "People, people everywhere, long lines, hysterical children and much confusion and anxiety as everyone was checked for disease—they pushed us around like cattle."

For some, like Ole Blindheim, a Norwegian who arrived with a friend in 1908, the experience was different. Blindheim wrote, "We came to Ellis Island. We were thinking America in high tones when we saw that Statue of Liberty. Our order was to roll up our sleeves, which we both did. Outside of that, we were just ordered to go right on. On both arms, I had three big marks of being vaccinated. They saw that, that was enough."

ARRIVAL

Arriving in the new country was a never-to-be-forgotten moment. Isaac Polvi came from Finland in 1894; his parents had arrived earlier. He described the anticipation he felt.

I t was evening when our ship arrived in New York. It didn't dock but stayed out [in the harbor].... I spent the entire night on deck watching the thousands of lights of the city. I thought: This is the land I've traveled to. Here I'll find my father, my mother and my new sister. What will my young life change into in this new world? I sat and meditated the entire night long and didn't even try to go to bed.

Many Scandinavian immigrants went to the Midwest. In the 1850s steamboats carried them along canals, rivers, and the Great Lakes. Travel could be hazardous. In 1852, Erik Thorstad of Norway traveled from Quebec to Milwaukee. In a letter, he described a disastrous collision.

W e left Buffalo on a large steamer, called the *Atlantic*.... The total number of passengers was 576, comprising 132 Norwegians, a number of Germans, and the rest Americans.

Since it was already late in the evening and I felt very sleepy, I opened my chest, took off my coat and laid it, together with my money and my watch, in the chest. I took out my bed clothes, made me a bed on the chest, and lay down to sleep. But when it was about half past two in the morning I awoke with a heavy shock. Immediately suspecting that another boat had run into ours, I hastened up...to the top deck, and then I was convinced at once that the steamer must have been damaged, for many people were lowering a boat with the greatest haste.... As the boat had taken in water on being lowered, it sank immediately and all were drowned.

Thereupon I went down to the second deck, hoping to find means of rescue. At that very moment the water rushed into the boat and the engines stopped. Then a pitiful cry arose. I and one of my comrades had taken hold of the stairs which led from the second to the third deck, but soon there were so many hands on it that we let go, knowing that we could not thus be saved. We thereupon climbed up to the third deck, where the pilot was at the wheel. I had altogether given up hope of being saved, for the boat began to sink more and more, and the water almost reached up there. While we stood thus, much distressed, we saw several people putting out a small boat, whereupon we at once hastened to help. We succeeded in getting it well out, and I was one of the first to get into the boat. When there were as many as the boat could hold, it was fortunately pushed away from the steamer. As oars were wanting, we rowed with our

The Thingvalla Line was a Danish ship company that transported people to the United States. The passengers here are about to dock in Hoboken, New Jersey, around 1895.

hands, and several bailed water from the boat with their hats. A ray of light, which we had seen far away when we were on the wreck and which we had taken for a lighthouse, we soon found to be a steamer hurrying to give us help. We were taken aboard directly, and then those who were on the wreck as well as those who were still paddling in the water were picked up....

The misery and the cries of distress which I witnessed and heard that night are indescribable, and I shall not forget it all as long as I live. The number of drowned was more than three hundred, of whom sixty-eight were Norwegians.

In 1864, 14-year-old Christiane Aldous traveled with a group of other Danish Mormon immigrants in a wagon train from Wyoming, Nebraska, to Salt Lake City, Utah. In her journal, she described the 1,100-mile journey, which took 10 weeks.

The first of the country was the rolling plains of Nebraska which were covered with...buffalo grass. The road was crude, just a rutty, dusty, winding, seemingly endless pair of ruts through which those before us had labored.... When we reached the Platte [River] the prospects of fording the river were appalling.... In the first ford the entire oxen and the wagon were lost. The driver barely escaped with his life.... Sudden rainstorms often fell on the weary travellers, drenching them and turning the road into a sea of mud that was sticky as glue.... It was grueling work to get through. Every morning the travelers rose early, women to prepare breakfast, wash dishes, pack for the march, while the men yoked the oxen.... Every spiral of smoke away from the camp, every sound, every cloud of dust meant a potential enemy—the Indians or a possible buffalo stampede. At night...a few miles more westward, we gathered around the campfire for...services and songs before climbing wearily into makeshift beds.

As Others Saw Them

A Norwegian magazine reported the reaction a group of Norwegian immigrants caused in Boston around 1840.

In Boston these newcomers occasioned considerable surprise. Few had heard of Norway, and the inhabitants [of Boston] came in throngs to the wharves to see the ship on which were emigrants from the high north. The foreign language of the emigrants, their clothes, and their customs were marveled at, but the visitors were even more astonished to find that people who came from a land so near the ice region as Norway looked like other human beings! They thought that men and women alike would be clad in skins from head to foot, that they would eat raw meat and, like the Eskimos, drink oil.

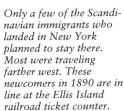

Only a few of the Scandinavian immigrants who landed in New York planned to stay there. Most were traveling farther west. These newcomers in 1890 are in line at the Ellis Island railroad ticket counter.

Immigrants, such as these on the Montana prairie, used horse carts and covered wagons to carry their possessions to new homesteads.

3000 LABORERS
WANTED

On the LAKE SUPERIOR AND MISSISSIPPI RAILROAD from Duluth at the Western Extremity of Lake Superior, to ST. PAUL.

Constant Employment will be given.   Wages range from $2.00 to $4.00 per Day.

MECHANICS
Are Needed at Duluth!

Wages to Masons and Plasterers, $4.00 per day; Carpenters, $3.00 per day.

10,000 EMIGRANTS

WANTED TO SETTLE ON THE LANDS OF THE COMPANY, NOW OFFERED ON LIBERAL CREDITS AND AT LOW PRICES.

Large bodies of Government Lands, subject to Homestead Settlement, or open to Pre-Emption. These Lands offer Facilities to Settlers not surpassed, if equalled by any lands in the West. They lie right along the line of the Railroad connecting Lake Superior with the Mississippi River, one of the most important Roads in the West. Forty miles of the Road are now in running order, and the whole Road (150 miles) will be completed by June, 1870. WHITE and YELLOW PINE, and VALUABLE HARDWOOD, convenient to Market, abound.

The SOIL is admirably adapted to the raising of WINTER WHEAT and TAME GRASSES. Stock have Good Pasture until the Depth of Winter.

The waters of Lake Superior, in connection with the Timber, make this much the warmest part of Minnesota. The navigation season at Duluth is several weeks longer than on the Mississippi. The LUMBER interest will furnish abundant and profitable WINTER WORK.

FREE TRANSPORTATION over the completed portion of the Railroad will be given to Laborers and all Settling on the Lands of the Company.

At Duluth Emigrants and their families will find free quarters in a new and commodious Emigrant House, until they locate themselves, by applying at Duluth to LUKE MARVIN, Agent. Laborers will report to WM. BRANCH, Contractor of the Road. For information as to Steamers to Duluth, inquire at Transportation Office in any of the Lake Cities.

DULUTH, MINN. JUNE 14, 1869.   "DULUTH MINNESOTIAN" PRINT.

Most immigrants wanted to find jobs, and some were swayed by posters plastered all over to attract laborers. This 1869 broadside tried to lure people to Duluth, Minnesota.

Many Icelanders landed in Quebec and made their way to the United States from there. Gunnar Johanson, who left Iceland in 1905, described the difficulties he had traveling.

By the time we got to Quebec I was very sick. I had a fever of 102 degrees. Later I found out it was scarlet fever, but I didn't know that then. I must have caught it while I was in Liverpool, because it takes about ten days for the sickness to show. I didn't want to let them know at the port in Quebec that I was sick, because I was afraid they wouldn't let me land, so I walked past the Immigration man and tried to stop myself from shaking. We had to go to a hotel there overnight until the train was ready to leave, and when we went out to catch the train we found it had gone two hours before. So we had to wait in the station and it was cold there and wet. We had to wait all afternoon for the train. When we got on I hardly knew what I was doing. I went and layed down on the berth, and for two days, three days, I couldn't eat and hardly drink. The boy who came from Iceland with me gave me a little water. That was all I wanted.

We got to Winnipeg and went to stay one night with a woman my mother had known, a women from the old country. And the next day we had to get the train to go to the United States. It had been raining for days and we had to walk knee-high through the water. I was shivering and shaking, so I hardly knew what I was doing. We got on the train and came down here and got off in Grand Forks, North Dakota.

My mother had written to a family we knew from the old country, and I was to go to be a hired man on their farm. It was a homestead they had taken out years before. The farmer met me at the station and took me to his house, but I was so sick by then I went right to sleep. His family and his children nursed me. They were good people. The daughter of the house, who was twelve then, took special care of me. I didn't notice her much then because I was sick and so young, but that's the girl I married when we both were older. They got a doctor out, Dr. Lax. He wasn't a real doctor; he was an Icelander who knew about medicines and things like that, and he gave me some pills and by and by I got better.

In 1907 the Swedish government established a Commission on Emigration to study the reasons Swedes emigrated and what happened to them in the United States. A man identified as E. C. S., who emigrated in 1871, described to the commission the difficulties of getting from New York to Chicago.

I ...landed in New York on 4 May. Now I was at last in the promised land, without family, without friends, and almost without money. Here I wandered back and forth like a deaf-mute. I had a ticket to Chicago and now set off for there, and then through some mistake of the railroad personnel I was sent the wrong way, so that I had to stay alone over a Sunday at Niagara Falls. There I got locked in the station house from Sunday morning to Monday morning. I showed my ticket to a hackney [horse-drawn cab] driver and he took me to another station, from which I got a seat to Chicago. Here there were cries from all sides: Come along to the Emigrant Home, but I had been warned about Chicago's emigrant runners, so I followed no one but took my knapsack and went off alone without knowing where. After wandering around for a while I caught sight of a sign on which there was written: Carl XV's Hotel [Carl XV was Sweden's king]. I went in there and was well received by a Smålänning [a former resident of Smålän, Sweden].

Irja Laaksonen came to the United States from Finland in 1907, when she was only four years old. Along with her mother, two brothers, and a sister, she was going to join her father, who had left for the New World the previous year. In her autobiography, Echoes from the Past, *Laaksonen described meeting him.*

My earliest memory of America is seeing the great Statue of Liberty. It was thrilling even for a little child. We landed at Ellis Island where we were detained for several days before being allowed to enter the country.

It was a beaming Papa who met our train when we finally arrived in Fitchburg [Massachusetts]. Finnish people usually do not approve of kissing and hugging in public. But when Papa saw Mama, he squeezed her so tightly that all she could do was laugh and say, "No, no, no!" Then Papa shook hands with my brothers and lifted up me and my little sister for a big kiss....

In Fitchburg Papa found work as a baker [his work in Finland] and also as a director of plays among the city's Finnish immigrants. The plays were produced at the Finnish Hall. After a year of hard work, he managed to save up enough money to pay for our tickets to America. Papa rented an apartment for us in a building next door to the Finnish Hall. Then he bought some furniture on the installment plan.

How well I remember that furniture! There was a rocker, a chair, and a sofa colored with green and black velvet flowers. The rug was tan with great big pink roses. When my brother Ilmari saw the furniture for the first time, he jumped up and down and shouted, "We're rich now! We're rich now!" Papa must have been very amused, knowing that the furniture was still a long way from being paid for.

Frederika Bremer was a Swedish feminist and writer. After touring the United States in 1849 and 1850, she wrote a book in which she made an interesting forecast.

What a glorious new Scandinavia might not Minnesota become! Here would the Swede find again his clear, romantic lakes, the plains of Scania rich in corn, and the valleys of Norrland; here would the Norwegian find his rapid rivers, his lofty mountains, for I include the Rocky Mountains and Oregon, in the new kingdom; and both nations their hunting fields and their fisheries. The Danes might here pasture their flocks and herds, and lay out their farms on richer and less misty coasts than those of Denmark.... The climate, the situation, the character of the scenery, agrees with our people better than that of any other of the American States, and none of them appear to me to have a greater or more beautiful future before them than Minnesota.

Around 1900, these Swedes found the place on the prairie where they wanted to live—Kansas.

FIRST IMPRESSIONS

Lars Henrik Henrikson and Gustava Nilsdotter Henrikson were photographed shortly after they arrived at their new home in Boelus, Nebraska, in 1881. It was their first picture taken in the United States, and they dressed up for the occasion. Gustava's gloves with no fingers were the style of the day. The Henriksons brought with them from Sweden their six children and a future son-in-law.

Johannes Nordboe was born in Norway in 1768 and came to the United States in 1832, as a relatively old man. He wrote a letter to the editor of a Norwegian newspaper describing his happiness with his life in Illinois.

Here no restrictions are placed upon the right to earn one's living. Here no monopolies and privileges reign. The farmer can sell his product freely without being accused of forestalling the market. Nor can one be charged for four driving horses when only one has been used.... Any person who is able to do so may manufacture goods of any kind, and may dispose of his goods in town or country without complaint, for there are no guilds to place restrictions upon diligence and industry....

Religion is free [in America] as it was when the Creator made man. Every man believes what he thinks right, and neither monks nor ministers have any influence in such matters. In the districts where I have been, an agreement is made between the pastor and the congregation whenever a vacancy occurs, and, as there are plenty of candidates, the demands of the ministers are moderate. Usually they are humane men; they never abuse anyone from the pulpit, [even] though he...never go to church. A poor man need never work for a minister without pay; such things belong only to the old world. Tithes [a fraction of one's income, usually 10 percent, owed to the state church in Scandinavian countries] do not exist.

Elizabeth Koren came to the United States from Norway and settled in Iowa with her husband, Ulrik Vilhelm Koren, a Lutheran minister. She described the experiences of her first year in America in her diary.

CHRISTMAS EVE, 1853. This was a strange Christmas Eve, indeed: so different from any I have ever known before. Here we were, Vilhelm and I, separated for the first time from relatives and friends, in a little log cabin far inland in America. For supper we had spareribs and coffee. As we sit here now, we get a little light from a lead dish in which there are tallow scraps and a little rag for a wick, placed on an overturned salt container.... Here is our dinner.... It consists of—*tykmelksuppe* [thick milk soup], boiled potatoes and ham. Here we sit then, we two at Vilhelm's little table...with a napkin for a tablecloth, a tin dish for a soup tureen and bowls instead of soup plates....

SATURDAY, JANUARY 7.... The dishes here vary from boiled pork to fried pork, rare to well done, with coffee in addition (milk when we can get it), good bread and butter. To this are added now and then potatoes...fried onions once in a while, and above all, the glass jar of pickles. That is our meal, morning, noon and evening.... Oh that I had some new potatoes and a little mackerel from home! It is really boring, this constant puzzling over tiresome food.... But the watermelon! It is extremely juicy and refreshing...bright red inside. You should see how people eat one big melon after another....

I believe that I shall reconcile myself.

In his autobiography, The Making of an American, *Jacob Riis recalled his first day in New York City in 1870.*

I made it my first business to buy a navy revolver of the largest size, investing in the purchase exactly one-half of my capital. I strapped the weapon on the outside of my coat and strode up Broadway, conscious that I was following the fashion of the country. I knew it upon the authority of a man who had been there before me and had returned, a gold digger in the early days of California; but America was America to us. We knew no distinction of West and East. By rights there ought to have been buffaloes and red Indians charging up and down Broadway. I am sorry to say that it is easier even to-day to make lots of people over there believe that, than that New York is paved, and lighted with electric lights, and quite as civilized as Copenhagen. They will have it that it is in the wilds. I saw none of the signs of this, but I encountered a friendly policeman, who, sizing me and my pistol up, tapped it gently with his club and advised me to leave it home, or I might get robbed of it. This, at first blush, seemed to confirm my apprehensions; but he was a very nice policeman, and took time to explain, seeing that I was very green. And I took his advice and put the revolver away, secretly relieved to get rid of it. It was quite heavy to carry around.

Thorstina Walters told the story of her father, an immigrant from Iceland who landed in Canada with a group of friends. Later, he moved to the Dakota Territory, where he met and married Thorstina's mother.

My father, Thorleifur Jóakimsson, came several years earlier than mother, in 1876, landing in Quebec, then proceeding on to the Icelandic settlement on the shores of Lake Winnipeg. One incident en route from Quebec to Manitoba that [he and his friends] often told about was the stop they made in Kingston, Ontario, where they had been told that they were to dine at the expense of the Canadian government. They entered a spacious, well appointed dining room, only to discover after they had partaken of the meal, that they and not the [Canadian] Dominion government, were to pay for it. The immigrants rushed out as fast as they could, until only the interpreter was left inside to argue with the innkeeper, his wife and servants, who then shut the door. Such action looked suspicious to one of the Icelandic immigrants, a man of prodigious strength. He voiced his protest, saying, "They shall not get away

Helga Lehtonen Pulkkinen, a young Finnish woman, had her photograph taken soon after she arrived in Peabody, Massachusetts, in 1905. From about 1890 to 1920, more single women emigrated from Scandinavia than single men.

with killing Halldór in there while I am around." He gave the door a push, making it fold up like paper, overthrowing the fat innkeeper who had his back to it. His wife made dire predictions as to the future of the Icelanders in America, and there the matter rested.

Ole Bull, a wealthy Norwegian violinist, bought about 140,000 acres of land in Pennsylvania around 1850 in order to start a utopian community for poverty-stricken Norwegian farmers. By the end of 1852, some 250 settlers had accepted his offer of free land. Though Bull gave concerts in Europe to raise funds to support the settlement, it failed within two years. Even so, Norwegian Americans today regard Bull as a hero, and a festival in his honor is held every year in Potter County, Pennsylvania.

Ida Lindgren emigrated from Sweden with her husband and five children and a small group of Swedes. Their destination was a little settlement near Manhattan, Kansas. In her travel diary, she wrote unhappily of the prairie.

What shall I say? Why has the Lord brought us here? Oh, I feel so oppressed, so unhappy! Two whole days it took us to get here.... We sat on boards in the work-wagon, packed in so tightly that we could not move a foot and we drove across endless, endless prairies.... The closer we came to Lake Sibley the more desolate the country seemed and the roads were altogether frightful, almost trackless. When we finally saw Lake Sibley at twelve o'clock at night, it consisted of four houses, two larger ones and two small, very small, as well as two under construction. The rooms Albinson had written he wished to rent us were not available but we were quartered here in Albinson's attic. The attic is divided into three rooms but with no doors; I have hung up a sheet in front of our "door." When I immediately asked, after we arrived, to go up with the children and put them to bed, there was no table, no chair, no bed, *nothing*, and there we were to stay! I set the candle on the floor, sat down beside it, took the children in my lap and burst into tears. I feel about to do so now too, I cannot really pull myself together and the Albinsons appear quite uncomfortable every time they see me. The Indians are not so far away from here...and all the men you see coming by, riding or driving wagons, are armed with revolvers and long carbines, and look like highway robbers.

Axel Jarlson came to the United States from Sweden with his sister in 1899. Like many other Scandinavians, he settled in Minnesota, where he wrote his first impressions of his new country.

One thing I like about this country is that you do not have to take off your hat to people. In Sweden you take off your hat to everybody you meet, and if you enter a store you take off your hat to the clerk. Another thing that makes me like this country is that I can share in the government. In Sweden my father never had a vote, and my brothers never could have voted because there is a property qualification that keeps out the poor people, and they had no chance to make money. Here any man of good character can have a vote after he has been a short time in the country, and people can elect him to any office. There are no aristocrats to push him down and say that he is not worthy because his father was poor. Some Swedes have become Governors of States, and many who landed here poor boys are now very rich.

Aarre Lahti came with his mother from Finland in 1912. His father had sent them ship tickets for the Titanic. *But Aarre's mother had to postpone her departure because she was having trouble disposing of the family furniture. That saved them from disaster at sea. Finally they reached Ironwood, Michigan, in the Upper Peninsula of that state.*

My first impression of Ironwood was formed while sitting in mother's lap in the vestibule of Saipa's Saloon [a Finnish American bar]. We had been brought there from the Chicago and Northwestern's railroad station to wait for father.

So, here sat mother, a teetotaler (as was father), among the odors of stale beer watching the men tramping to and from the barroom. The sawdust-covered floor was sprinkled with cigar and cigarette butts. The ever-present spittoon was surrounded by brown spatter.

We sat for a long time before father could be contacted at the Scott and Howe Sawmill. During this anxious wait, I had been assuring mother that I would recognize father. But when father finally appeared, I screamed at the sight of the stranger reaching for me.

Eventually we reached a cluster of houses around Norrie Mine. After climbing the creaky stairs to father's attic rooms, mother broke the tall feather of her hat on the slanting attic walls. This, and the contrast between the cosmopolitan capital city of Helsinki and this frontier mining town, she never forgot.

Gretchen Yost came to the United States from Sweden in 1919 with her mother and brother.

I remember when we landed, squirming through all the grown-up people to see the Statue of Liberty. I had [bought] my first pair of shoes and they were button-up high shoes and somebody stepped on them and I spit on my shoes [because] I wanted them to be so shiny. I remember when we were met at the station at Porter, Indiana. It was my first car.... I leaned out, I wanted everybody to see me. I thought, "Are you looking at me? I'm in a car!" And I had a funny little round hat, a little tweed hat, and my long braids. I don't think anyone realizes the excitement of a new country. Today, of course, I'm very thankful; it's been my country.

Hulda Belin landed in Canada in 1908 and boarded a train to Minnesota. Years later, she recalled a haunting incident.

So the train continued on and we were in Michigan, U.S.A., and then into Minnesota's snowy wastes. The train made a stop and off of the train climbed a youth; he was tall and gangly, 18 or 19 years old, and you could see that he was Swedish. Not a person was to be seen at the stop, that little square wooden house. He stood there alone and as though lost. He had no overcoat and it was cold. No one was in sight to meet him and no dwelling houses were to be seen. Then the train went on and he stood there alone. I have often wondered what his fate was.

Bishop Hill

The Swedish settlement at Bishop Hill, Illinois, marked the beginning of Swedish American immigration in the 19th century. It was founded by Erik Jansson, a self-styled "prophet" who had attacked the state-sponsored Lutheran Church of Sweden. Accused of heresy, Jansson fled to the United States in 1845. The following year, about 1,200 of his followers joined him.

Conditions were harsh for the new settlers. During the first winter, they lived in earthen "houses" dug out of the hills. But Jansson had ambitious plans. He had surveyors lay out a town with parks, a hospital, a school, and a central square with a church. Jansson planned the settlement as a utopian community, in which everyone would share equally in the property and possessions.

For a few years, Bishop Hill thrived. A successful collective farm was organized, and the settlers built a town with bricks made by women. In the town hall, called Big Brick, were a kitchen and dining room with room for hundreds of people. Carpenters, blacksmiths, shoemakers, tailors, and others contributed to the colony's support. New colonists continued to arrive from Sweden. By 1850, the colony's land had grown to 14,000 acres.

But when an epidemic of cholera broke out in 1849, many settlers died, including Jansson's wife and two of his children. The next year Jansson was murdered by a disgruntled colonist.

The colony elected trustees to take Jansson's place. But without his leadership, the people began to quarrel among themselves. In 1861, the collective community was formally dissolved. Yet most of the settlers remained in the area, and some of their descendants live there today. Several of the original buildings are still standing.

One of the few surviving photos of members of the Bishop Hill Settlement.

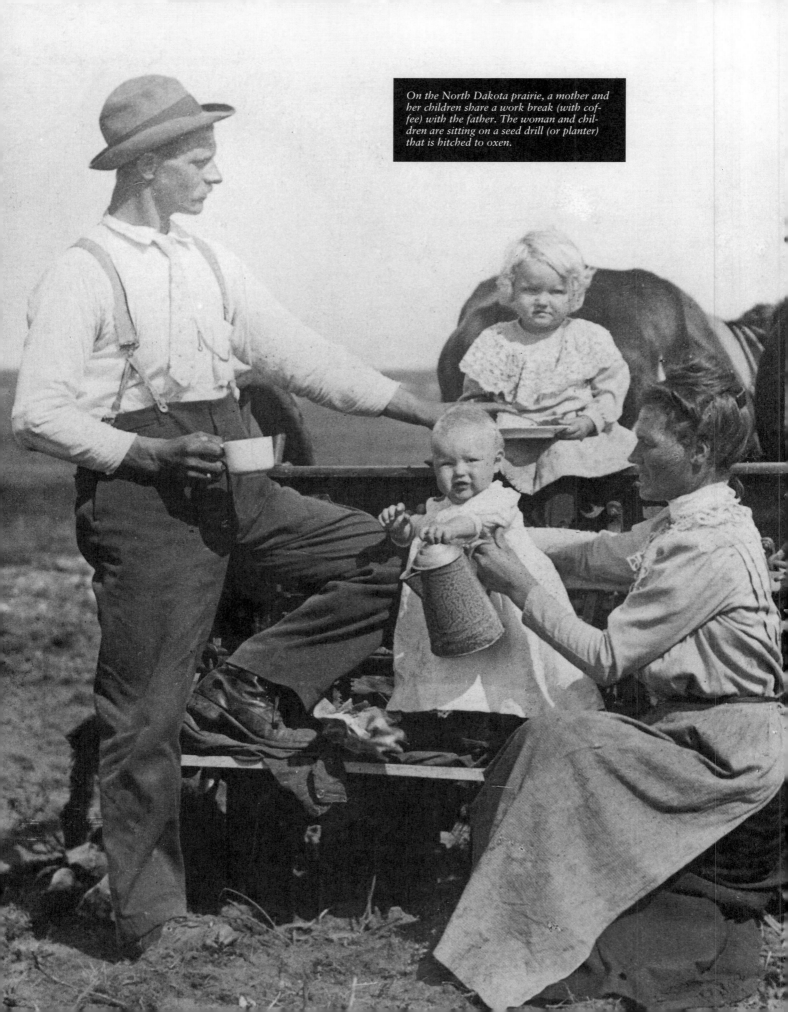

On the North Dakota prairie, a mother and her children share a work break (with coffee) with the father. The woman and children are sitting on a seed drill (or planter) that is hitched to oxen.

CHAPTER FOUR

FINDING A JOB

To the Scandinavians, one attraction of the United States was its seemingly endless fertile farmland. Gjert Gregoriussen Hovland, who settled in Illinois in 1836, described it as "a Land of Canaan...which produces so richly without fertilizer that Norway can no more be compared to America than a desert to a garden of herbs in blossom."

Many of the early Norwegian immigrants obtained land that had never been farmed. Sometimes it was difficult for the settlers just to get to their new homesteads, which they knew only as marks on a map.

A. O. Houkom related the struggles of the Norwegian pioneers north of LaCrosse, Wisconsin, in 1852: "There was no trace of a path; they had to clear a way through the brush, make long detours because of rivers, and build bridges across creeks in order to get over with oxen and wagons."

The Scandinavians did not mind the hard work because in most cases work was what they came for. Besides, as Ole Andersen wrote to his family in Denmark in 1889, working in the United States was different: "Over here it's not at all like back home. Nobody has to hire himself out for a year at a time, only for a month. If a worker wants to quit, he doesn't have to tell his

employer in advance. He can just leave when his time is over, and the farmer can't come into town after him. This is a free country. Nobody is bound like back home."

The California gold rush of 1849 attracted prospectors from all over the world; Scandinavians were no exception. A few Danes, however, had already lived in California when it was still part of Mexico. Peter Lassen, a blacksmith from Copenhagen, helped to blaze a trail from Missouri to Oregon in 1839. Mt. Lassen in northern California is named for him.

After the gold rush, some of the Scandinavian prospectors settled in California to raise crops, build ships, or open stores and other businesses. Jon Thoreson, born in Telemark, Norway, started an overland mail service between Utah and California. Known as "Snowshoe Thompson," Thoreson carried mail across the Sierra Nevada Mountains for almost 20 years.

Wherever Danish American farmers settled, they concentrated on the production of eggs and dairy products. Danes often introduced new farming technology. Christopher Nissen, who arrived in Petaluma, California, in 1864, purchased an incubator that hatched eggs more efficiently than hens did. As a result, Petaluma became the center of California's poultry industry. Another Danish immigrant, arriving in Iowa in 1882, brought

the first mechanical milk separator in the United States.

Many Swedish immigrants, following in the wake of the Norwegian pioneers, settled in or near existing Norwegian American communities in Illinois and Minnesota. Before long, the more numerous Swedes began to form their own communities, spreading across Minnesota and into the Dakotas, Kansas, and Nebraska.

Swedish immigrants often joined the pick-and-shovel gangs that paved the roadbeds for the Western railroad lines. James J. Hill hired thousands of Swedes to build railroads from St. Paul and Chicago to the West Coast. Hill supposedly said, "Give me Swedes, snuff, and whiskey, and I'll build a railroad through hell."

After the railroad work was done, Swedes bought land along the tracks to start farms. Some Swedes settled in places outside the Northwest and Midwest. S. M. Swenson, who immigrated to Texas in 1838, brought Swedish contract laborers to work on his immense Lattarp ranch. Some of the Swedish Texans began to grow cotton, a crop that must have been unfamiliar to them at first.

Many Scandinavians fought in the U.S. Civil War, primarily on the Union side. John Ericsson, a Swedish immigrant, designed the *Monitor,* an iron-plated warship with a revolving gun turret. Although people scoffed at the "cheesebox on a raft," it proved its worth in 1862 against the much larger Confederate ironclad ship *Virginia*. Other *Monitor*-class ships helped the North maintain its blockade of Southern ports.

W. W. Thomas, a native of Maine who went to Sweden in the 1870s as an American diplomat, encouraged Swedes to emigrate to his home state. Thomas founded the settlement of New Sweden in the forestland of northern Maine. Besides developing a logging industry there, Swedes planted one of their favorite foods—the potato. Today, Aroostook County remains one of the nation's major potato-producing regions. And there are still Swedish-speaking people in the county.

In California, the Swedes of Fresno County helped make the Sun-Maid Raisin Growers one of the leading producers of that product. In Alaska, Swedish immigrant farmers pioneered the development of agriculture in the Matanuska Valley. By 1920, Swedish Americans owned more land in the United States than all the arable land of Sweden itself.

Scandinavia's forests had long provided a living for its people. Many Norwegian immigrants found work in logging camps in Wisconsin, Michigan, and Minnesota. Swedes and Finns went to Maine, Washington, Oregon, and California. Crosscut saws were nicknamed "Swede fiddles." Some farmers spent the winters at logging camps to earn much-needed cash—leaving their wives to maintain the farms and raise the children. Logging was dangerous work; according to one account, the only safety regulation was "run or die" when a tree came down.

Scandinavians found that the forest-covered northwest United States reminded them of home. By the 1880s, Swedes, Norwegians, and Danes had settled all along the Pacific coast. In Washington and Oregon, they went into the lumber and shipbuilding industries.

Having lived close to the sea in their native countries, Scandinavians on the Pacific Coast flocked to the fishing industries. Norwegian immigrants introduced a kind of fish trap that they had used in Norway. Scandinavians found work in

Many Scandinavians were lumberjacks, like these men in Price County, Wisconsin. After work, they enjoyed the accordion music that accompanied dancing and singing.

the salmon fisheries and canneries of Oregon. They also pioneered the fishing industry in Alaska.

Mining was another trade that many Scandinavians had learned at home. Norwegians found work in the copper and iron mines of Michigan and in the lead mines of Wisconsin.

Finnish American miners also worked in Michigan. The opening of iron mines in northern Minnesota in the 1890s brought an influx of Finnish American miners. Other Finns went farther west, to Wyoming, Utah, and Montana. Some settled in New England, where they worked in cloth mills and other kinds of factories.

Women in Scandinavia traditionally shared the work, perhaps because centuries ago when their Viking husbands left on long journeys, the women had to run the farms. In frontier settlements in the United States, women sheared the sheep, carded the wool into strands, and wove it into cloth. They milked the cows and churned the milk into butter, a staple of Scandinavian cooking. After the trees were felled, women chopped and pulled up the roots that held the stumps in the ground, "so that the earth flew around them," one pioneer remembered.

In the late 19th and early 20th centuries, more Scandinavian single women arrived than single men. They often found work as domestic servants in urban areas. Scandinavian women were in demand for such jobs because of their reputation for cleanliness and their cooking abilities. Many women also worked in the textile mills of New England.

Men also took factory jobs, of course, but many Scandinavians were skilled carpenters and stonemasons. They entered the building trades in such major cities as Chicago, Minneapolis, Seattle, San Francisco, and New York.

Swedes who arrived in Chicago just after the great fire of 1871 used their skills to rebuild the city. Lars G. Hallberg, a graduate of a Swedish architecture school, played a major role in planning a new Chicago. Many other Swedes designed the buildings, headed the construction companies, and built the skyscrapers, hospitals, hotels, schools, banks, and houses that made Chicago the nation's second-largest city. By 1930, according to one estimate, one-third of the houses in Chicago had been built by Swedish American companies.

At the time most Scandinavian immigrants arrived, socialism was a powerful political force in the Scandinavian countries. Many immigrants believed in socialist ideals. Scandinavian American miners and other workers became active members of the labor movement in the United States. From 1895 until 1916, Scandinavian American mine workers joined strikes in Idaho, Montana, Colorado, Minnesota, and Michigan. All the strikes were crushed, generally with the help of state governments that supported the mine owners.

Some Scandinavian Americans backed the most radical American labor organization of the time. This was the Industrial Workers of the World (IWW), whose members were nicknamed "Wobblies." The IWW, founded in 1905, wanted to organize all workers into "one big union."

A Swedish immigrant called Joe Hill (his birth name was Joel Hägglund) wrote many of the songs that the IWW used to raise the spirits of its members. In 1914 Hill was charged with the murder of two Salt Lake City shopkeepers during a robbery. A jury convicted him, and he was sentenced to death by firing squad. Despite President Woodrow Wilson's request that Utah's governor reconsider the case, Hill was executed.

In 1916, the IWW took the lead in organizing a strike by the iron miners of Minnesota, most of whom were Finnish. Although the strike was called off after three months, the mine owners granted wage increases.

The following year, the United States entered World War I. President Wilson called for an end to all strikes while the conflict lasted. The IWW, which opposed all wars, continued to organize strikes and job actions. State militias and local vigilantes invaded the homes of IWW members. Some were jailed; others were tarred and feathered or run out of town.

In Butte, Montana, the vice president of the Anaconda Mining Company explained why the company fired about 400 Finnish American workers. "Finlanders," he declared, were "known trouble makers."

To suppress opposition to U.S.

Icelandic Americans display part of the salmon catch on their fishing boat at Point Roberts, Washington.

involvement in World War I, Congress passed an Espionage Act and a Trading with the Enemy Act. These made it illegal to encourage "disloyalty." They provided penalties "for acts or utterances considered damaging to U.S. foreign policy." Two Finnish American editors of a socialist newspaper were sent to jail because their bookstore had one copy of a book entitled *War, What For?*

The Scandinavian nations were neutral in World War I. Even so, Scandinavian Americans suffered from wartime prejudice against German Americans. The use of Norwegian, Swedish, Finnish, and other Scandinavian languages was discouraged because it was an indication of "foreign sympathies." Iowa, to cite an extreme example, banned anyone from speaking on the telephone in any language except English.

Soon after the war ended, the United States Attorney General launched further attacks on people suspected of socialist and communist sympathies. During the "Red Scare" of 1919–20, thousands of people were arrested and held in jail without being charged with a crime.

By no means were all Scandinavian Americans supporters of the IWW or of socialism. In fact, many communities split bitterly over the issues raised by social reformers. But Scandinavian Americans as a group became targets of antiforeign bigotry and the postwar Red Scare.

Finnish immigrants endured one kind of prejudice that other Scandinavians did not. Classified as "Asians," they were sometimes barred from obtaining citizenship. A federal law, passed in 1790, allowed "any alien, being a free white person" to become a naturalized citizen. (In 1873, the law was amended to include those "of African nativity or descent.") Asian immigrants could not become naturalized citizens—though their children, born in the United States, were automatically citizens.

In 1908 John Svan and 15 other Finns were denied citizenship by District Attorney John C. Sweet of St. Paul, Minnesota. Svan appealed to the U.S. District Court. In the case *John Svan* v. *United States*, Judge William A. Cant officially declared that though the Finns were originally from Asia, they "are now among the whitest people in Europe." That settled the issue.

FOREST AND SEA

This was said to be the largest load of logs ever pulled by two horses. Its height was more than 33 feet and it weighed 144 tons. Destined for the 1893 Chicago World's Fair, it took nine railroad flatcars to carry it into the city.

Members of all the Scandinavian groups were involved in logging. A Danish immigrant wrote home in 1872 describing his work in the rapidly growing lumber town of Manistee, Michigan.

We are paid thirty-five dollars a month plus board. The work consists of felling trees, sometimes with axes, sometimes with saws. The tools are so well designed and light that a boy of sixteen or eighteen can do the work as well and earn as much as a man of twenty or thirty. The only regrettable thing here is the law or rule that says no wages can be paid between 1 November and 1 June. But we can get everything on credit from the mill owners, who all sell all kinds of wares.... We now work from 6 A.M. until 6 P.M. with an hour off for lunch. The food that we get at the restaurants and from the mill owners is extremely good. Those who cook for themselves are paid a food allowance of fourteen dollars a month. An entire family can live respectably on that sum, even if it consists of six or eight persons. Firewood is free. Pork costs about ten cents per kilogram, beef about twice that much. Butter is thirty to fifty cents per kilogram, which eggs cost thirty six cents a dozen. Cotton clothes are much cheaper than in Denmark.

William Ahl's father was a Finnish immigrant who settled in Gardiner, Massachusetts. Ahl described the exploitation of the workers by the lumber companies.

My father became indentured as a lumberjack to a company in Maine. They paid his railroad fare to the lumber camp, supplies, food, and rough barracks shelter for the crew, but he would receive no pay until all expenses of the trip, the housing and food were met. Work days were long and life in camp primitive and miserable. So after a short time, he and another Finn walked out of the wilderness after midnight and headed back to Massachusetts, traveling at night to avoid capture by the detectives hired by the lumber company to return workers to the job.

Logging was a highly dangerous occupation. The aviator Charles Lindbergh described how his Swedish immigrant grandfather suffered an accident.

One day he stumbled, and fell against the spinning saw. Its teeth cut through his arm near the shoulder and ripped open his back. The belt hurled him halfway across the shed. The mill hands claimed that the gash was so deep they could see my grandfather's heart beating. They bound

Playing cards was one of the activities of loggers in their free time. This picture was taken at a logging camp near Puget Sound around 1900.

his wounds up crudely and sent for the minister, Reverend C. S. Harrison. Minister Harrison had my grandfather laid on some hay in the bottom of an oxcart and hauled him, bleeding terribly, over the rough roads to the family cabin. A man was started off on the only horse available, with instructions to get relays wherever he could and rush a doctor back. But the nearest doctor lived at St. Cloud—and he was not at home. The messenger eventually found him in a still more distant village, helping a young wife give birth to her child. Meanwhile my grandmother, the minister, and the friends who came to help expected Grandfather to die. They washed his wounds with cold water from a nearby spring, picked out rags and sawdust, and tried to stop the flow of blood.

Three days passed before the doctor arrived. He amputated the arm and stitched together the gaping hole in the back. My grandfather lived despite shock, infection, and loss of blood. Lying on his bed, in great pain, he demanded to see his left arm before it was buried in the garden. It was brought to him in a small, rough-board coffin. Taking the fingers in those of his right hand, he said slowly, in broken English, "You have been a good friend to me for fifty years. But you can't be with me any more. So good-by. Good-by, my friend."

It took months for my grandfather to recover. Then, he had special tools fashioned for his single-handed use.

John W. Anderson, the grandson of a Norwegian immigrant, grew up on a farm about 200 miles northwest of Milwaukee. He described his father's work in the timber industry.

In the spring of the year he followed the log drives. These drives took place when the rivers were swollen from melting snow. Men like my father were skilled at riding the logs down to the sawmills. When a log was held up on some

Even with six men wielding saws and axes, it took nearly a day to fell the giant trees of the Northwest. These men worked in Washington state in the early 1900s.

This lumber camp in Cable, Wisconsin, employed many Finnish men; Finnish women often worked as cooks in these camps.

obstructions a log jam piled up. It was then the task of the drivers to find the key log that was causing the jam. Finding this log was difficult and dangerous work. When the jam was broken hundreds and sometimes thousands of logs shot forward down the river. Breaking a log jam resulted in injury and death to many drivers.

Gunnar Johanson came to the United States from Iceland in 1905. After working on a farm in North Dakota, he looked for a job in a lumber camp. He described the reason for the change.

After a while I thought I'd like more money, more cash to spend. I wanted to save up to get a farm of my own. So I decided to go lumbering. I worked in the woods for thirteen winters, cutting down trees and logging and chipping and all that. There's some hundred men working in the camps. You work all day, hard work. It's a rough life, you know, in the camps. You work all day and play cards every night until nine. Then the lights went out. First it is hot around the stove, then the stove would go out. Before morning you were pretty near frozen stiff, because there was nobody firing the stove. We had just a couple of boards to sleep on with some hay on them.

Mary Anderson was born in Sweden in 1873 and moved to Michigan when she was 16. She would later become an important labor organizer. Anderson recalled one of her jobs.

I got a place in a lumberjack's boarding house washing dishes. It was very hard work.... I got two dollars a week and my board and lodging. We had to carry water and look out for fifteen or twenty lumberjacks. It was early morning work—and all-day-long work. There was a cook and two other women for housecleaning, making beds and laying the table, but

I didn't know much of the language and I had nobody to talk to. It seemed to me that there was nothing in my life but dirty dishes to wash and a kitchen to clean up.

In 1870 a small group of Icelanders established a settlement on Washington Island in the northwest part of Lake Michigan. Many carried on their ancestral skills in fishing. One wrote a letter home in 1872 that described working conditions.

I have been four days out on the ice fishing and have caught fifty fish, so far, and have sold them for nearly seven dollars; people come here to buy the fish and take it to nearby places; it sells at four cents a pound. There are many fishermen here from the communities around; they live in small cabins during the fishing season, and leave when the ice shows signs of breaking. When several days pass without anyone coming to buy, they put their fish side by side; no one takes from another a single fish; some days one catches thirty, others none.

John Kuivala moved to Astoria, Oregon, from Finland in 1910 when he was 18. He worked in both the lumber and fishing industries. He remembered his experiences in the latter.

I was fishing. My uncle, he had a boat with another man. And then 1911, he got this motor boat. That's the time they start to get the motor on the fishing boat; there were sails before. And I went to fish with him on the [Columbia] River. And, oh, that was a good year! I paid my bills and everything.

Fishing season started first of May and lasted four months till the 25th of August, except you'd take off the river six o'clock Saturday night and then you'd have to start fishing again on Sunday night six o'clock. Two men on the boat, twenty-six footers. They were independent fishermen. Pretty near all the canneries paid the same price. Woman worked there, lots of Finnish woman. They were filling, putting the fish in the can. They were called fillers....

Summertime, I went fishing, Bristol Bay, Alaska. First time in 1919. I fish over there in the summertime, and then wintertime I went longshoring. Nineteen thirty-two, I quit. That was the last year I was up in Alaska, 1932. Most of the time when

After the catch is in, the fish are mounted on a scaffolding to dry. Before the days of refrigerated railroad cars, much of the catch was dried before being shipped to markets.

Crew members furl the mainsail on Star of France, *a fishing ship heading into anchorage on the West Coast in 1919. Scandinavians had been seafarers since the days of the Vikings.*

As Others Saw Them

For some reason every Swede heads for the lumbering centers as soon as he arrives in this country and he is a fixture around lumber camps and sawmills. He knows no English, has no money, can neither read, write nor talk so anyone can understand him, but he has an unfailing instinct to work for himself. He will take any kind of contracting job so long as he doesn't get paid by the day. In thirty days he can ask for snuff and eighteen different kinds of food in English, he has made more money out of his contract than six American laborers working alongside him, he can sign his name on a paycheck, he yodels a wild mixture of English, Swedish, Esperanto and profanity...and has figured out an intricate system of Scandinavian trigonometry and American arithmetic that beats the paymaster's calculating machine a dozen ways when it comes to figuring out what he has coming on his contract.

—*journalist Paul Hosmer in* Now We're Loggin' *(1930)*

you were fishing, you have to live on the boat, except Sunday. That was closed season on the Sunday there, too. When they open the boat, most of the time it rain and rain and rain, cold rain, and no chance to dry your clothes. Nothing. *Ja*, that was miserable.

Margit Johnsen was born in a town in Norway north of the Arctic Circle. Her father was a fisherman. She moved to Tacoma, Washington, in 1925, when she was 24. Johnsen later described her work as a young woman in the Alaskan fishing industry.

I was working with the herring. You take the guts out of it and salt it. It is hard work and salting, it's hard on your hands. This was 1926, in southeastern Alaska. They called the herring camp Big Port Walter; it's close to Port Alexander. There was one Englishman and the rest of them was all Norwegian. The cook, he was Swedish.

When I had been there about two weeks...one of the fellows in the kitchen, he didn't like it, so he went down [to the lower forty-eight states]. They were three in the kitchen; there was about seventy men to cook for. We were fourteen girls and I got picked to work in the kitchen out of fourteen. I was tickled pink, and got good pay. Then I had monthly wages. There didn't turn out to be much herring for a long time and all the girls got sent down. I got to stay then; because I was in the kitchen. So I had the advantage of that. All I did, was took care of the dishes when they were all through and saw to it that all the vegetables were taken care of, ready to cook. Then when I come down in the fall in 1927, then I got married. So I didn't go up anymore.

Gustav Simonson came to the United States from Norway in 1923. Eventually he settled on the Pacific coast and then Alaska. He described his work in the fishing industry.

I took the steamer to Juneau, Alaska. Middle of the winter, with a chunk of salt pork and a few potatoes. Very few dollars, I think I had twenty-some dollars when I took off. When I started fishing, we got two and a half cents a pound for halibut. You know that you wasn't going to get rich in a hurry, but anyway you were going to make a living. I've been fishing ever since.

Halibut boats were relatively small boats, three men, four men; that was what they call a mosquito fleet. We in the Juneau fleet hardly ever fished outside the island at that time, mostly inside the island. You were out ten days. Every ten days or two weeks, you were back in again. You bait and you haul and you dress and you ice. You have a line that is three hundred fathoms long and at that time, you have probably 115–120 hooks. You set them down on the bottom, anchor on each end in a buoy. We would leave it out for many hours, overnights. You haul that back up again. Sometimes you got lots of fish, sometimes you didn't get so many.

Workers channel salmon into a canning factory in Puget Sound for processing. The picture was taken at the beginning of the century by Anders Wilse, a Norwegian photographer who worked in Seattle and documented the activities of that community before returning to Norway in 1901.

The Icelandic crew of the Penguin, *a fishing boat in Washington State.*

Teams of horses helped these loggers in Washington transport the wood from the forest.

Finnish longshoremen are ready for work in Astoria, Oregon, around 1915. Astoria was known as the "Helsinki of the West."

MINING AND RAILROADS

Prospectors pan for gold in the Yukon Territory in 1898. Hopes of striking it rich drew Scandinavians to mining sites all over the West and Canada.

Jens Storm Schmidt emigrated to Texas in 1846, when he was 27. Three years later he became one of the thousands who headed for California, hoping to make a fortune in the gold rush. He wrote this letter to his parents in Denmark.

U pon arriving in Sacramento, my first question was how far it was to the gold mines, and was told fifty kilometers.... I bought the food I needed, built myself a gold machine (which is like a cradle), loaded my horses, and departed. When I got there I saw several people wriggling their machines and watched them for a while. The place is ugly. Small and large stones have been cast aside. Under them is some red soil, which one puts into a bucket and carries to the machine, which must be close to the water. I pitched my tent and began my new profession as a prospector. Ha, ha, ha, who would have believed I would become a prospector? The first day I tried it I wasn't able to find anything. The next couple days I found a little, but not much the first week. The next week I worked only four and a half days because it rained, but I made 240 Danish dollars, not bad for a beginner.

The western railroads encroached on the lands inhabited by Native Americans, and railroad workers feared being attacked by them. August Andrén, an immigrant from Sweden, described an incident in western Nebraska in 1867.

W e still had not seen any Indians although we knew that we were in the Sioux Indians' territory, but we were not sure of our scalps and one evening as we were sitting around the campfire, we heard a rustling some distance away which gave us a real fright.

"Put out the fire!" Schwartz commanded.

"Get rid of your pipes," whispered the Knalle.

"God damn it, be quiet," urged Ollie.

I, for my part, looked for my revolver, but Rundbäck considered this much too reckless...and when I aimed at where the rustling was still coming from and asked if it was friend or foe—now he would have to look out for himself for I would shoot—the Norwegian grabbed a chunk of firewood and said that if I could not keep my mouth shut he would help me, for here it was no use to show one's daring but rather to commit oneself to the care of the Almighty and act friendly, for we could not manage a fight with the Indians. Well, there we sat and listened to the rustling in the dry leaves and did not know whether it was Indians or wild animals, but later at night it became quiet and sleep overcame us.

These fire fighters worked for the Quincy Mining Company in Michigan. Some of the men carry gas masks because fires in the mines created suffocating fumes.

Around the mining camps, prospectors used gold dust to pay for goods. This store used a tiny scale to weigh the dust and calculate its value.

When we woke up and investigated the place, we found a very large rat that had made off with a hunk of pork, had made all the noise in the leaves, and then had finally eaten itself to death on it.

After arriving from Denmark in 1870, Jacob Riis took a variety of jobs before becoming a newspaper reporter. He once worked as a coal miner at Brady's Bend on the Allegheny River, as he recalled in his autobiography.

You did not go down through a shaft, but straight in through the side of a hill to the bowels of the mountain, following a track on which a little donkey drew the coal to the mouth of the mine and sent it down the incline to run up and down a hill a mile or more by its own gravity before it reached the place of unloading. Through one of these we marched in, Adler and I, one summer morning with new pick-axes on our shoulders and nasty little oil lamps fixed in our hats to light us through the darkness where every second we stumbled over chunks of slate rock, or into pools of water that oozed through from above. An old miner whose way lay past the fork in the tunnel where our lead began showed us how to use our picks and the timbers to brace the slate that roofed over the vein, and left us to ourselves in a chamber perhaps ten feet wide and the height of a man.

We were to be paid by the ton, I forget how much, but it was very little, and we lost no time getting to work. We had to dig away the coal at the floor with our picks, lying on our knees to do it, and afterward drive wedges under the roof to loosen the mass. It was hard work, and entirely inexperienced as we were, we made but little headway. As the day wore on, the darkness and silence grew very oppressive, and made us start nervously at the least thing. The sudden arrival of our donkey with its cart gave me a dreadful fright. The friendly beast greeted us with a joyous bray and rubbed its shaggy sides against us in the most companionable way. In the flickering light of my lamp I caught sight of its long ears waving over me—I don't believe I had seen three donkeys before in my life; there were none where I came from—and heard that demoniac shriek, and I verily believe I thought the evil one had come for me in person. I know that I nearly fainted.

Norwegians work on the railroad track in Peterson, Minnesota, in 1896. The town of Peterson was Norwegian, founded by an immigrant.

Lillie Hill worked at the forge as a blacksmith's helper, heating rivets for the Southern Pacific Railroad yard in Portland, Oregon. She learned the trade as a young woman in Finland.

Miners pick at underground seams in a mine near Bisbee, Arizona, in 1915. A strike in Bisbee's copper mines in 1917 was crushed when vigilantes rounded up strikers, most of whom were Finnish, and drove them out of the area.

That donkey was a discerning animal. I think it knew when it first set eyes on us that we were not going to overwork it; and we didn't. When, toward evening, we quit work, after narrowly escaping being killed by a large stone that fell from the roof in consequence of our neglect to brace it up properly, our united efforts had resulted in barely filling two of the little carts, and we had earned, if I recollect right, something like sixty cents each. The fall of the roof robbed us of all desire to try mining again. It knocked the lamps from our hats, and, in dumbness that could almost be felt, we groped our way back to the light along the track, getting more badly frightened as we went. The last stretch of way we ran, holding each other's hands as though we were not men and miners, but two frightened children in the dark.

Isaac Polvi, who moved from Finland to the Upper Peninsula of Michigan in 1894, wrote about the hazards of copper mining.

Many men were killed in accidents in the mines every day. There were hundreds of men around the mine offices looking for work. Mike Rossu [Polvi's best friend] and I decided that there might be something for two boys to do, so we went to the Tamarack mine around noon one day. There wasn't any activity at the No. 2 shaft house, so we went in. The shaft was simply a vertical hole in the ground. Vapor enveloped the shaft opening, but an occasional breeze would clear it momentarily. In the mist we could see the steel cable moving, indicating that someone was ascending the shaft. We waited. A man emerged from the vapor. Then he went back in and returned with the headless body of a miner. Other men appeared with another body. One carried the first man's head by the hair. Mike and I followed them. An undertaker came and sewed the man's head back on to his torso. Then the two bodies were placed in long baskets and taken away. Mike and I ran home and told everyone how the two bodies were brought up from the Tamarack mine.

One of the men who was looking for work said, "This means that there is work for two men." These poor fellows were in competition for the jobs that had been held by the slips; or they were forced to work in the most dangerous places in the mine—so that they could be sent to the surface as corpses. There were always men who were willing to take the places of the dead.

Once a small-time boss said, "You have to load several cars now." The place he indicated was unstable. Falling rocks made the men reluctant to enter the area. "If you won't do what I tell you, what are you doing here?" said the boss.

I had to go there with a truck and wait while the trammers filled the cars. Suddenly a slab of rock broke loose from a tunnel roof and fell on edge, cutting a man through at the shoulder. I ran over to him and removed the rock. His heart was exposed and still beating, but not for long. I took hold of him under his arms, and his Finnish partner came to help. We dragged him clear first thing, because we knew more rocks would fall. We put him on two boards in the truck and pushed him to the shaft.

The boss was there and accompanied us to the surface in the cage. We took the man out of the cage, and the boss immediately ordered us to go back down into the mine.

I showed him my clothes. I was covered with blood. "We won't go back," I said, "until after we've washed our clothes and they have dried."

The boss followed us to the changing room. "I'm short-handed," he said, "and I have to get that spot cleaned out."

"Go in there yourself," we told him, "and take the dead man for a partner. We'll come back tomorrow evening."

"You don't need to come at all," he said.

I said, "We'll be back tomorrow evening to work. You forced the men to go into that section. You're a murderer, and I can prove it. I know what I'm talking about."...

I worked there for three years and was witness to many tragic events. I felt that my young life suffered because of mine work.

Peter Kekkonen left Finland for the United States in 1905, when he was 16 years old. He moved to northern Minnesota, where he hoped to farm. To make money for his own place, he worked at an iron mine.

So I went to work in an iron mine—the Mesabi iron range, the biggest in the world. Maybe you've heard of it. I got two dollars a day for my work and I paid fifteen dollars a month to an old Finnish woman who ran a boarding house, so that I was able to save a little. But the work was hard and it was dangerous. We went down in a shaft. Nowadays that iron mine is all open pit, but then we went down in a shaft. There were no electric lights in the mine then, not even any carbide lamps. We had no candles. The air was bad because there was only one shaft, so there was no movement. We were coughing all the time, all of us. And the iron dust got in our lungs. Plenty of young men I knew died of silicosis from that mine in later years. Even the candles wouldn't burn well in that air. For some reason, one candle wouldn't burn alone; if you had two candles close together, they would burn. One alone was no good. So that's the way we always used them— two together.

Conditions in the mine were bad in other ways, too. The roof was not propped up tight, so there were many rockfalls. One time I was working with two friends in a deep section of the mine and there was a rockfall. All the top seemed to come down on us. The candles went out and everything was black. After a long time, some men came to us from the other part of the mine, and when it was light I saw that my two friends were dead.

The job seekers [for the mines] were always told, "Presently there are no jobs available as there have been no deaths or injuries."

—*Matti Pelto, a Finnish American immigrant who started work in the Minnesota mines in 1908*

Many Finns immigrated to the Upper Peninsula in Michigan and worked in the copper mines. John Laitin, at right, is at the ground level of a Hancock mine around 1910.

A woman here can support herself and her husband rather well on her earning, without his earning anything, for that is what I have been doing ever since I came here.

—from an 1871 letter sent to Sweden from Stina Wiback in Chicago

Many Scandinavian women who came to the United States on their own found jobs as domestic servants. Selma Marie Toivenen (at right) and a friend worked in homes in Massachusetts. Toivenen came from Finland in 1891.

WOMEN'S WORK

Many Scandinavian women came to America alone and had to find jobs. Jannicke Saehle arrived in Wisconsin in 1847. She wrote her brother in Norway about her new life in the United States.

I have worked at a hotel for five weeks, doing washing and ironing; and I enjoy the best treatment, though I cannot speak with the people [because she did not know English]. I have food and drink in abundance. A breakfast here consists of chicken, mutton, beef, or pork, warm or cold wheat bread, butter, white cheese, eggs, or small pancakes, the best coffee, tea, cream, and sugar. For dinner the best courses are served. Supper is eaten at six o'clock, with warm biscuits, and several kinds of cold wheat bread, cold meats, bacon, cakes, preserved apples, plums, and berries, which are eaten with cream, and tea and coffee—and my greatest regret here is to see the superabundance of food, much of which has to be thrown to the chickens and the swine, when I think of my dear ones in Bergen [Norway], who like so many others must at this time lack the necessaries of life.

I have received a dollar a week for the first five weeks, and hereafter shall have $1.25, and if I can stand it through the whole winter I shall get a dollar and a half a week, and I shall not have to do the washing, for I did not think I was strong enough for this work.

Maren Lorensen immigrated from Denmark to Racine, Wisconsin, in 1893. Two letters to her friend Stine in Jutland show her progress from employee to business owner in five years' time.

Oh I wish you were over here; oh, there would be so much to talk about; oh, what a fine time we would have. I have no one here I can discuss things with like we could.... I work at a children's home now; I have been here for a month. I and another Danish girl wash and iron constantly; we do nothing else. The work is hard as long as it lasts, but we also have a lot of time off. We have all of Friday and Saturday off, and we can also get a little spare time every day. We never work later than 6 o'clock, and we are also often finished before then. Then we go for walks.... I earn a good wage here, and I really need that as I am greatly in debt now because I was sick. It cost me 100 *kroner* [about $20] as it is expensive to go to the doctor over here, but I do like being here because it is so good to be your own master. When we are finished with our work, we can come and go as we like; we can go out or lie down whenever we want; no one ever calls us or tells us to do anything. I get 3 dollars and 25 cents a week. [August 9, 1893.]

We [Maren and her sister] finally found a house in the spring, and we have washed and ironed and mangled [pressed]

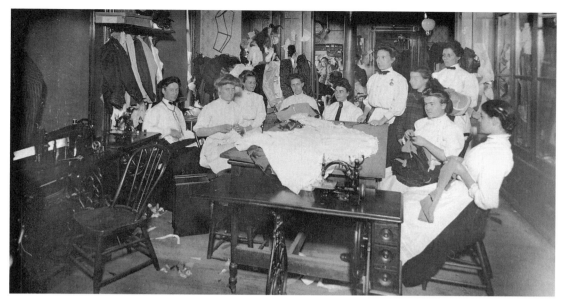

Most Scandinavian women had sewing skills, and many found work as dressmakers. The Norwegian women here work in a fashionable dress shop in St. Paul, Minnesota, around 1890.

ever since, and we have been busy the whole time. I now usually earn about 20 *kroner* a week; yes, I have even earned as much as 24 and that is after all the expenses, and they add up to quite a bit. We pay 37 *kroner* a month for rent, and then I must pay for food and fuel, soap and starch and all that kind of thing, so you can see that I earn quite a lot every week. Perhaps you do not believe me, but every word I write to you is true.... We have a washing machine; they are not like those back home, and a wringer and a mangle, and we have water in the house; all we have to do is turn it on. [September 29, 1898.]

Anna Ohlson came to the United States from Norway in 1906 as a little girl. Her family settled on the Dakota prairie. She recalled the work she did before she married.

When I got to be about sixteen I went away to work on a cook car [for migrant farm workers]. You go around with the thrashing team and cook food for them as they go from farm to farm. The thrashing crew chief hires you. There's lots of fun in that, you know. Lots of work, but lots of fun. There's young boys, men, from all different countries there. French Canadians, Norwegians, Americans. One woman and I did all the work. We'd get up in the morning before it was light and start the stove up and give them breakfast. We had to give them a meat-and-potatoes breakfast. Of course, we had something [food already prepared] we could warm up, otherwise we'd be up all night. We had a table and chairs, benches, and we'd set about sixteen at the table. Then about ten o'clock we'd carry lunches out to the field to them—sandwiches and doughnuts and coffee. And then, of course, the big meal at noon. And then another lunch about three—sandwiches and coffee and cake, maybe. And then another big meal at night. And in-between times we'd wash the dishes and do the cooking. We were busy. But, you know, it was fun. They'd help us in the evening with the dishes and there were a lot of young

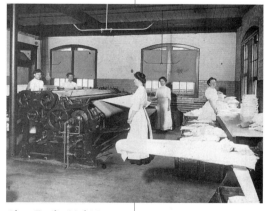

Alma Emilia Maki (at center) with her coworkers at a Worcester, Massachusetts, hospital. She is mangling, or pressing, sheets.

people, so there was a lot of laughing and joking. And the thrashing crew moved from farm to farm, so we got to see different places.... The cooks were paid the same as the men—four dollars a day—but there were two of us, so we had to divide it. We made more money than we would with housework. That was the only other work women could do there.

Evelyn Crookhorn was the daughter of Swedish immigrants. She grew up in New York, where both her parents were "in service," domestic servants in wealthy homes. She told an interviewer about their experiences.

Both my parents worked for George F. Baker, who founded National City Bank. They traveled with these people to Newport [Rhode Island] and Deal, New Jersey, and Florida in his own private railroad car.

They stopped after I was born. The woman [Baker's wife] was so fond of mother, she came to visit when I was a baby, and my mother told me she was ashamed because all the diapers were drying on the line in the kitchen. There was such a difference between the way the lady was living and my parents lived....

They used to follow the society pages. They would see Mrs. Whitney and Mrs. Payson [wealthy society women], and they knew all the dirt about them, like who had an abortion and who did this and that. When my mother and aunt and father got together, they would giggle and laugh about all the antics of these people. They really enjoyed all those days. You know, they were all young. They didn't look upon being servants as demeaning. They considered it an honor. To be in service, as they called it, was wonderful.

Some enterprising women ran boardinghouses. The work was long and hard. Velma Antilla Koven, the daughter of Finnish immigrants, described her mother's work at the family boardinghouse in Raymond, Washington.

Mamma was just five feet tall but she could lift a hundred-pound sack of flour onto her shoulders and carry it six steps up to the kitchen where she had a big wood range with three ovens and a huge griddle. She had to get up at 4 A.M. to fire the stove since wood (not gas) was the fuel used and the loggers had to have an early breakfast which usually consisted of mush (oatmeal), bacon, eggs, toast, pancakes, syrup, jam, and coffee.

The dining room had six square tables each seating eight people. The men brought their dishes to the metal-covered kitchen table after breakfast. Each then picked up his lunch bucket which was always in the same spot. After breakfast Mamma and her workers, the dishwasher and waitress, went upstairs to make the beds.

On washdays, the towels and pillowcases were boiled in a huge kettle on top of the stove but the sheets were sent out to be laundered. Mamma hand-scrubbed the towels and pillow cases! Ironing the pillow cases and the sheets was done after

These Danish women work at Jensen Creamery in Salt Lake City, Utah.

Students at the Swedish Hospital School of Nursing in Minneapolis in 1903. Scandinavians, like other immigrant groups, contributed funds to form social service organizations like hospitals, orphanages, and homes for the elderly.

lunch. Her chores eased considerably when we bought a washing machine.

After the room chores, Mamma would put a pot roast on the stove and then start baking the pies, cakes and *pullaa* [coffee bread laced with cinnamon and cardamom]. Pies were made daily but cakes and *pullaa* were usually made only once a week.... After baking the pies, Mamma and her helpers made the sandwiches for the next day's lunch buckets carried by the logger to the jobs.

The mill workers ate lunch in the boarding house. Lunch (or dinner as it was called then) consisted of steamed potatoes, pot roast, two vegetables, salad, bread and butter (including hardtack), coffee, milk, buttermilk, and pie. The diners helped themselves to the food from the serving dishes placed on the tables. Each could eat as much as his heart (stomach?) desired! The waitresses kept the serving platters full. Even so, we served fewer people at lunch than at breakfast or supper....

Supper, also an "eat all you desire" meal, was served in the kitchen. The desserts were laid out on a table which the men might eat at their leisure during the evening. Hot coffee was always available from the pot on the stove. Each boarder, however, had to wait on himself.

The cost for all this food? Room and board was $28 a month! Breakfast, if bought separately, was 25 cents, dinner or supper was a little more—35 cents. And if a boarder missed a meal, Pappa would deduct the amount from the monthly bill.

Mamma's work wasn't done even though the boarders were enjoying the evening dessert. She had to prepare for the next morning's breakfast by slicing the bacon from a big slab. She would lay the slices into big pans to be put into the ovens in the morning and she had to prepare the pancake batter before retiring. Her day—seven days a week—started at 4 A.M. and ended at 11 P.M. but I never heard her complain about the long hours. She had no vacation because she didn't like to be away from the boarding house.

A Swedish woman in Washington State displays her handiwork. Flax was spun into linen threads and then woven into tea towels or other products.

Some single women homesteaded alone. Norwegian immigrant Carrie Einarson posed in front of her new home in Inland, South Dakota, for this photograph that she sent to a friend.

It took a lot of strength to break the tough grassy turf that covered the earth on the Great Plains. Often, the only implements were hand tools, like the hoe used by Eric Braarud, a Norwegian immigrant clearing his land in Polk County, Minnesota.

FARMERS AND PIONEERS

Many Scandinavian immigrants of the mid-19th century dreamed of owning their own farms. In 1861, Danish-born Andreas Fredericksen Herslev wrote a letter describing his efforts to start a farm in Wisconsin.

Last year I planted six bushels of wheat, one and a half of rye, two and a half of barley, ten of oats, four of peas and a little over an acre of millet. I let part of my land lie fallow with timothy grass because grain prices are low and it is more profitable to raise cattle. Besides, I have no desire to plant more grain than Johanne [his wife] and I can harvest. We have butchered and sold two pigs that weighed two hundred kilograms together and have eight left, which we intend to butcher during the course of the winter. Pork is cheap, though, so we got only about six dollars per one hundred kilograms. We also have ten cattle. They are cheap, too; a good cow is worth fifteen to twenty dollars. But horses are expensive because of the war [the Civil War]. I have thought about buying a mare, but will wait until prices go down.

Right now is a good time to emigrate to America. Those who have families will be able to buy food cheaply until they can grow enough to support themselves. Single men will be able to make good money next summer, because the government has drafted most of the men into the army.

Axel Jarlson came from Sweden with his sister Helene in 1899. Like many Scandinavians, he settled in Minnesota, where his brothers and sisters were living. He described the work of clearing the land for his first farm with the help of a French Canadian named Joachim.

We took two toboggans loaded with our goods and provisions, and made the ten-mile journey from my brother's house in three hours. The snow was eighteen inches deep on the level, but there was a good hard crust that bore us perfectly most of the way. The cold was about ten below zero, but we were steaming when we got to the end of our journey. I wore two pairs of thick woolen stockings with shoe-packs outside them—the shoe-pack is a moccasin made of red sole leather, its top of strong blanket; it is very warm and keeps out wet....

So we lived till near the first of April when the sun began to grow warm and the ice and snow to melt. In that time we chopped about nine acres and made forty-five cords of wood, which we dragged to the bank of the river and left there for the boats to take, the storekeeper giving me credit for it on his

Cooperation was a necessity in the farming communities. A barn raising—like this one near the Rainy River in Minnesota around 1900—provided an opportunity for getting work done, but it also left time for socializing.

books at $1.25 a cord. We also cut two roads through the bush. In order to haul the wood and break the roads I had to buy an ox team and bob sleigh which I got with harness, a ton of hay and four bushels of turnips for $63. I made the oxen a shelter of poles and boughs and birch bark sloping up to the top of an old tree root.

By April 15 the ground which we had chopped over was ready for planting, for all the snow and ice was gone and the sun was warm. I bought a lot of seed of several kinds, and went to work with spade and hoe, among the stumps of the clearing, putting in potatoes, corn, wheat, turnips, carrots, and a few onions, melons and pumpkins....

About the first of June my sister Helene came with a preserving kettle, a lot of glass jars and a big scheme. We got a cook stove and a barrel of sugar, and put a sign on the river bank announcing that we would pay 50 cents cash for 12 quarts of strawberries, raspberries or blackberries. All through June, July and August Indians kept bringing us the berries, and my sister kept preserving, canning and labeling them. Meanwhile we dug a roothouse into the side of the hill and sided it up and roofed it over with logs, and we built a log stable for cattle. A load of lumber that we got for $2 had some planed boards in it, of which we made doors. The rest we used for roofs, which we finally shingled before winter came on again....

We raised almost all our own provisions after the first three months.... I have no trouble selling my produce, as the storekeeper takes it all and sells it down the river.

Both women and men shared the arduous farm work. Here, Norwegian farmers in southern Wisconsin used a thresher to harvest wheat in the 1870s.

Elise Amalie Waerenskjold left Norway and moved to Texas in 1847 with her husband. They settled on a ranch at Four-Mile Prairie. In 1857 she wrote to a friend in Norway.

You no doubt know that cattle-breeding is our main means of making a living. We do not plan to sell the cows, but only the steers until we can acquire about 200 calves a year. This spring we can expect about 70. Cows and calves are now $15 each, and a three-year-old untrained ox costs the same. When an ox is trained for work, it costs much more. We have five horses and a mule. The mule is unusually gentle and sure-footed. It is the children's and my "riding horse." Niels sits in my lap and Otto behind me. We do have a four-wheeled carriage but very seldom use it.

We have 62 sheep, and this month and next we are expecting many lambs. I help clip only one sheep while the others clip two. Wilhelm, my husband, can keep up with anyone. He is very quick at all kinds of work. I do not know how many pigs we have—not because we have so many, but because pigs are so difficult to keep track of.

Carl Johan and Fredrik Bergman also settled in Texas. They moved from Sweden to Brooklyn, New York, in 1879, but five years later they traveled with other Swedes to Travis County and took up farming. Two years after that, they wrote home about a terrible storm.

On June 19 we had quite a bad storm accompanied by hail, so that a large part of the crops were damaged, indeed almost everything was ruined, but luckily it did not hurt us. We had hail but not so much or so large, they were like small hen's eggs. In other places, however, they were like when you put both your hands together. That seemed big enough, but they had still bigger ones in other places. It sounds unbelievable but I don't doubt it, it must be true in any case: they weighed seven pounds and then you must believe they must have been big. Our house came near to being blown apart. Fred was inside when the storm started, he felt how the house began to give way in the wind and tried to get out but the door wouldn't open because of the way the house was leaning, therefore he had to jump out the window. I happened to be out in the outhouse, so I was not afraid. In other places the hail went right through the roofs and in many places livestock were killed.

Gro Svendsen came to the United States from Norway in 1862 as a bride with her new husband and his family. They settled on the prairie of Iowa. In a letter home, Gro described her new life.

There is the prairie fire or, as they call it here, "Faieren." This is terrifying, and the fire rages in both the spring and the fall. Whatever it leaves behind in the fall, it consumes in the spring, so there is nothing left of the long grass on the prairies, sloughs, and marshes. It is a strange and terrible sight to see all the fields a sea of fire. Quite often the scorching flames sweep everything along in their path—people, cattle, hay, fences. In dry weather with a strong wind the fire will race faster than the speediest horse. No one dares to travel without carrying matches, so that if there is a fire he can fight it by building another in this way save his life and prevent burns, which sometimes prove fatal.

Snakes are found here in the summertime and are also a worry to us. I am horribly afraid of them, particularly the rattlesnake. The rattlesnake is the same as the *klapperslange*. I have seen many of them and thousands of ordinary snakes.

Ida Lindgren moved from Sweden to Kansas with her husband, Gustaf, in 1870. She wrote home about farming on the prairie.

We have not had rain since the beginning of June, and then with this heat and often strong winds as well, you can imagine how everything has dried out. There has also been a general lamentation and fear for the coming year. We have gotten a fair amount of wheat, rye, and oats, for they are ready early, but no one here will get corn or potatoes. We have a few summer potatoes but many don't even have that.... Instead of selling the oats and part of the rye as we had expected, we must now use them for the livestock, since there was no corn. We are glad we have the oats (for many don't have any and must feed wheat to the stock) and had hoped to have the corn leaves to add to the fodder. But then one fine day there came millions, trillions of grasshoppers in great clouds, hiding the sun, and coming down onto the fields, eating up *everything* that was still there, the leaves on the trees, peaches, grapes, cucumbers, onions, cabbage, everything, everything. Only the peach stones still hung on the trees, showing what had once been there.

At the end of a busy season, workers gather around a steam engine on the Anders Hultstrand farm in North Dakota, with a grain elevator in the background. Farmers in the United States used modern equipment that was unknown in the Old Country.

Gutzon Borglum

John Gutzon de la Mothe Borglum was born in Idaho Territory in 1867. Three years earlier, his parents had come from Denmark with other Mormon converts. Even as a youth, Gutzon knew he wanted to be an artist. He recalled years later that his interests included Italian artists, Wild Bill Hickok, Sioux warriors, and Danish legends that his mother had told him.

Borglum's first major commissions were to sculpt figures for the Cathedral of St. John the Divine in New York City and a six-ton head of Abraham Lincoln for the U.S. Capitol in Washington, D.C. Then in 1915, a group of southern businessmen asked Borglum to carve a monument on Stone Mountain in Georgia. Borglum planned a mammoth sculpture of Confederate soldiers. But the project became embroiled in controversy and Borglum was fired. Before leaving the site, he destroyed his models so that future artists could not use his work. This so angered the Georgia commission that it swore out a warrant for Borglum's arrest and he fled the state.

By chance, some South Dakota officials wanted to create a memorial that would become a tourist attraction. They asked Borglum to look at the Black Hills. He and his son Lincoln climbed up the face of Mount Rushmore, and there, Borglum conceived the project that would occupy him until his death.

The work began in earnest in 1927 with the blasting of rock for the head of George Washington. With dynamite and jackhammers, the heads of four U.S. Presidents—Washington, Thomas Jefferson, Abraham Lincoln, and Theodore Roosevelt—emerged from the mountain during the next 14 years. The faces were 60 feet high. Borglum believed these men represented the spirit of America. At Borglum's death in 1941, the monument was virtually completed. His son directed the finishing touches.

Borglum plants a flag on Mount Rushmore before beginning work on the monument.

They are not the kind of grasshoppers we see in Sweden but are large, grayish ones. Now most of them have moved southward to devastate other areas since there was nothing more to consume here. Certainly it is sad and distressing and depressing for body and soul to find that no matter how hard one drudges and works, one still has nothing, less than nothing.

Cecil Hofteig remembered the homesteading of his grandfather, who moved from Iceland to Minnesota in 1878.

Wheat was the first crop my grandfather planted, and the next year he put in some oats. Later on he planted corn, but, as long as I can remember, he continued to raise wheat. He had sheep right from the start, and he always had cattle. For many years he had milk cows, not for a dairy business but for cream, which we separated and sold to a truck picking it up. We fed the skim to the calves, and we had some hogs too. Our farming was diversified.

The first years the wheat was taken down to Minnesota Falls...on the Minnesota River, northeast of us, where it was milled, and we traded it for flour. Taking wheat to Minnesota Falls by horse and wagon was a regular fall routine, and sometimes we hauled it by sleigh in winter.

I remember that our old granary, which is still standing, had an outside stairway, and at the top this stairway was a platform. I can barely remember men carrying bags of grain up that stairway and dumping them into the grain bin which had an upstairs and a downstairs. The bin downstairs was filled by pouring the grain through a hole in the upstairs floor. When the lower bin was full, we closed that off and started filling the upper bin, putting boards up against the door to wall it in. Everything was grain tight....

My dad then bought a John Deere grain elevator run by horses. No one else in the community had one, and it was borrowed often. I still have this horse power outfit. The shaft leading to the elevator was turned by horses hitched to a long lever running from a central gear arrangement. One horse could have done the work but our horses worked better together. Walking in a circle, they had to step over the shaft each time around. I wish I had a penny for every bushel that went up that elevator. The farmers borrowing it returned it in good condition. It was a real labor-saver.

Denmark modernized its dairy industry at the end of the 19th century. Immigrants such as Hans Hansen, who settled in Ferndale, California, in 1887, brought these improvements with them. Two years later, his wife, Sine Nygard Hansen, then seven months pregnant, wrote her mother a letter describing their life.

Early in the morning, at about 5 o'clock, we have to get up; sometimes we just want to stay in bed a little longer, but there is no help for it, we must get up and milk; the cows are loose in the field, so they first have to be driven into a corral. Before we finish milking the cows it is usually 7:30, and then I have to go in and make the fire and prepare some food for us; sometimes I make pancakes, the ordinary breakfast

Siri Rustebakke and her daughters spin wool in front of their home in Black Earth, Wisconsin, around 1873. Spinning was a feminine responsibility in farm families.

around here, or else I make some porridge, and afterward we always have to have coffee. I have also helped in the dairy with the skimming and washing up, but I do not do that all the time anymore. The rest of the day is taken up with all kinds of housework; there is no bread we can buy, I have to wash every piece of clothing myself, and it is the same in the house; it is not easy to get help here like it is at home. At 4 o'clock it is time to milk again, and when we are finished, we have supper and go to bed very tired.

Finns often turned to farming to escape the backbreaking, dangerous work in the mines. In 1910, Martin Kaurala was born in Mass City, Michigan, the son of Finnish immigrants. He described growing up on the family farm.

At the time of my birth, Father had lost his health in a very wet copper mine and, following the company doctor's recommendation, moved to a recently purchased forty-acre parcel of wooded land. The first winter of 1911–1912, our family lived in a tiny shack on an adjacent settler's land. Life was a constant struggle for survival: a hand-to-mouth life before more land could be cleared and made fit for raising hay, grain, potatoes, and other crops, and when more cows could be kept.

Hardships, poverty and long hours of toil were the order of the day for my parents, and as soon as their children became able to help, we had to pitch in according to our abilities. Father's brother loaned him the money for the final installment on the land contract; otherwise, we well might have lost our homestead.

As the eldest of two boys, early on I had no lack of work—helping to clear land, making hay, helping take care of the cattle, and other chores. Water had to be hand pumped and carried, and there was not always enough in the well....

I have pleasant memories of the early years when I went with Father by horse and wagon (or sleigh) to the logging camps in the hinterlands to solicit orders for, and later to deliver, hay, potatoes and rutabagas. Visitors to these camps were accorded the "open house" treatment. A bounteous lunch was always spread out on the long table, with cakes, pies, and cookies galore. And sweet

A Finnish family in their cornfield on a farm in Michigan. Even the youngest children did their part of the work as soon as they were able.

canned milk, not natural, for the coffee! I felt myself to be a very important person in those days when called upon to translate or to calculate something for Father.

On Saturdays were the weekly trips to Mass City, some four miles away, to bring firewood, butter, eggs, and sometimes meat products to the individual customers and to bring back the weekly supply of basic food commodities that had to be bought from our general merchandise cooperative store. On the occasions when a beef animal was slaughtered and Dad would peddle meat in town, I was there to translate and to figure out what the housewives owed for their meat purchases.

One of the earliest meat-selling trips stands out vividly in my memory. Dad had slaughtered a young pig, a springer, and we went to town to sell pork. We stopped at a group of homes before getting there, and I went to the railroad agent's house, that of a non-Finn, to say that my dad had "pig's meat" for sale. The kindly lady came to buy some and told me, "Young farmer, now when you get to the housewives in Mass City, you should tell them that our dad has some *nice young pork*, not pig's meat for sale. Come to our wagon to see it!" On the way to town I practiced this new sales pitch I had just learned. I could say it much easier in Finnish!

Thorstina Walters, the daughter of Icelandic immigrants who settled in North Dakota, recalled her home on the prairie.

My first fond memories of North Dakota are of the second house that my father built on the homestead on the Tongue River, Akra Township, Pembina County. The pioneer cabin with its sod roof was now abandoned. It had presented many problems to my mother. For instance: when it leaked, the only dry spot in the room was under the table, so she placed a box with me in it there for safekeeping. But this second house was of sturdy, hand-hewn oak logs with a red roof, the doors and window casings painted green. Inside and out the walls were always a gleaming white through frequent and liberal applications of whitewash. There was a lean-to of lumber that served as a kitchen. I have a mental picture of the large living room that formed the principal part of the house downstairs.... Through the window one saw two mighty oaks; between them mother had stretched her clothes line. These oaks were also mother's sun-dial, more reliable, in her opinion, than the clock for there was no mistaking the length of the shadows....

I also found the outside of our home most interesting. Toward the west was the barn and the corral where the cows were milked in summer. Near the corral were the serviceberry bushes; there the berries grew to wondrous size due to the abundant, rich fertilizer. To the southeast was the granary much used in summer by my grandfather when he cut the hops from the vines and spread them out to dry. Later these were sold at twenty-five cents a pound.... But the greatest interest in summer centered around my mother's milkhouse, north of the house. There were several well-made steps down to the door leading to it. One entered a cool, boarded room, with a small window above the door, a

A Danish family in front of their sod home in Custer County, Nebraska. Though the house was made of earth, a team of horses shows how sturdy the roof was.

scrupulously clean floor and broad white shelves on which the milkpans stood in imposing array with the thick cream on top, kept sweet for as long as three days in this subterranean wonder house. There were other things on these shelves that had a way of whetting the appetite, such as thick rounds of butter, covered with cheese cloth, delectable cheeses, including the *"mysuost"* made from whey, crocks with cheesecloth around the top through which the delicious *"skyr"* (cultured milk) was draining.

Kristina Carlson Johnson immigrated from Sweden to South Dakota in the 1880s. Her daughter remembered the importance of neighbors.

Often some neighbor would drop in, in the evening, visiting until a late hour. Then worrying about finding the way home, they would locate the North Star as a guide and go on from there. Mother would place the little kerosene lamp in the window as an added precaution. The popular means of motivation [transportation] in those days was on foot, often many miles, but as they were accustomed to that, it caused no worry.

On still evenings it was possible to tell just who of the neighbors was coming, or who was coming from town, or just how far away they were, by the particular rattle of the wagon or the clank of the harness or by the wheels bumping certain rocks. On dark evenings our little lamp was set in the window so that it could be seen from the road. In the cool of the evening, one could hear the neighbors urging their tired oxen on as they worked them until dark, trying to get their farming done.

Laurence Larson moved from Norway to Iowa with his parents in 1870. Years later he would become a historian, serving as the president of the American Historical Association. He wrote about the home his father built.

The site of the new homestead was a little knoll, near the top of which Father built his house. He dug into the hillside to a depth of about three feet and set his log construction above this excavation. It might therefore be called in part dugout and in part log house. The walls had been carefully plastered inside and the house proved to be a warm and

Some Finns, like the Suomela family, farmed in Maine. With their cousin Toivo (far left), the three Suomela sons, Wäino, Niilo, and Yrjö (from the left), dig for potatoes on their hilltop farm in Greenwood around 1925.

Ole Rölvaag

Ole Edvart Rölvaag was born in 1876 on a small Norwegian island, just south of the Arctic Circle. The settlement where he grew up was on a cove called Rölvaag. Later, after immigrating to the United States, he took this as his last name.

Young Ole had to walk seven miles to the island's school, which was open for only nine weeks each year. He left school at age 15 because his father told him that he was not worth educating. Even so, he devoured books from the local library, and when he heard that a village 14 miles away had a copy of the novel *Ivanhoe,* he walked there to get it.

Ole became a fisherman, like most of the other men in the community. During the long winter nights, he read books to the other fishermen. But he hated this lonely existence, particularly after many of his friends died in a storm. He wrote to an uncle in South Dakota, asking for a ticket to the United States. After two years, it arrived. Rölvaag landed in New York in 1896. He traveled by train to South Dakota for three days and nights, with only a loaf of bread to eat.

Rölvaag did not like farming any more than fishing, however. He really wanted to write, but his father's judgment of his abilities held him back. Finally, he enrolled in Augustana College in South Dakota, finding joy and success for the first time. He continued his studies at St. Olaf College in Northfield, Minnesota, where he later taught Norwegian and other subjects.

In college, Rölvaag wrote his first novel in Norwegian. Several more followed. The series was published in Norway in 1924 and 1925. Two years later it was translated into English and appeared as *Giants in the Earth.* Set in South Dakota, the story describes the experiences of immigrant homesteaders in the 1870s. An instant success, it has been called the best novel of the American immigrant experience. Two sequels were published, the second in 1932, the year after Rölvaag's death.

Rölvaag never lost his love for Norway. He criticized antiforeign sentiment in the United States during World War I and advocated that Norwegian immigrants keep as much of their heritage as possible. He helped to found the Norwegian-American Historical Association, which today continues the work of preserving and studying the contributions Norwegians have made to the United States.

comfortable dwelling. The room (for there was but one) was not large, about ten by sixteen feet. It was in every way like the usual pioneer cabin, except that it had three windows, while the number in the ordinary log house was only one or two.

The house was warmed by a little stove.... Otherwise the important furnishings were homemade. Father was reasonably skillful in the use of tools and in the winter he had much time to use them. We ate from a homemade table; we slept in a homemade bed. We sat on benches that my father had made, but the chairs that we had came from a store in town. We hung our wraps on wooden pegs which, for our purpose, were as good as hooks. In some of our neighbors' houses I saw wooden spoons, but our tableware, such as it was, came from the village store.

We used tallow candles for lighting purposes a part of the time, but most of our light came from a kerosene lamp. Once an old man who was skilled with a carving tool came to our home and made my sister and me each a pair of wooden shoes, of which we were inordinately proud. We had to make an immediate trip to our grandparents' house to display our new footwear. After a time the basswood split into pieces, however, and by that time our pride had also suffered a serious cleavage.

Ellen Larson, the daughter of Swedish immigrants, wrote a family history in which she recalled what it was like to live in a sod house.

The sod houses didn't last...so long and had to be replaced every so many years and you may be sure the ones Dad built were well made. They were cool in summer and warm in winter, the walls being about two feet thick. Some sod houses leaked muddy water when it rained and continued leaking muddy water after the rain was over with....

Our house didn't leak, but we had something else that happened, which was quite exciting. Fredulph [her brother] wasn't feeling well and was lying on the floor in the bedroom, when he gave an alarming call: "En orm! En orm!," that is, "A snake! A snake!" It had worked its way through the wall. After Dad got it out it was then he said, "That's it! Now we are going to build our new [wooden] house!" That was done in 1903.

Lettie Galby married Pastor Realf Ottesen Brandt at Lincoln Church near Ridgeway, Iowa, in 1883. Soon afterward, the couple moved to a community called Wood Lake in Dakota Territory. She described their first home there.

Our little kitchen was really so cold that winter that I often put on overshoes and tied a scarf over my head before preparing breakfast—even when I was going to bake pancakes. I had brought with me from home a number of jars of canned fruit and preserves. To my dismay I discovered one day that these were freezing. Several of the jars had burst and the precious contents were a total loss. We straightway carried all the jars up from the cellar and put them in the closet opening on the little bedroom. We also kept our potatoes and other vegetables in this closet that winter. There was an open well or cistern in the yard from which we could draw up water with a rope and pail. We used this water for mopping and cleaning. My husband warned me that it must not be used for household purposes until the well was cleaned out and put in better shape. In the meantime we obtained water for household use elsewhere.

I had strict injunctions not to try to haul up any water from this cistern while my husband was away. One day in his absence I was making the house spick-and-span against his return and needed more water. I thought I was able to manipulate the rope and pail well enough to get up some water, and went out to try it. I got up a pailful of water, and with it a very strange-looking object. It was an animal of some kind, very plump and fat, but quite foreign to me. I thought I had made a great discovery, and carefully put it away to show my husband on his return. Instead of being impressed by my "discovery," he was much chagrined that he had failed, after all, to keep from me the knowledge that the cistern was full of dead gophers!

Anna Ohlson immigrated to the United States from Norway in 1906 as a little girl. Her family settled on the Dakota prairie.

Sometimes we were snowed in. The snow would come up so high you couldn't see where the fences were. My father had to take a rope when he went out to the barn to take care of the horses and cows. The rope was so he could get back to the house through the snow when he was through. We were cut off one time for two weeks. Finally, my father went into town to get coffee and salt and hear the news. We really needed the coffee. My mother couldn't stand it without coffee. He went in and it was two days before he came back, because while he was in town another blizzard came up. But we got along all right. We had plenty of wood and we stayed warm and we did the work that had to be done.

We were luckier than one family that lived to the south of us. They came to settle in a new place and made a dugout in the side of the hill to live in while they built their house. It was just a young couple, a man and a woman. And I guess they didn't know how quickly winter came, because pretty soon the snow came and they still didn't have their house built, just the dugout with a blanket hanging for their door. They saw that they were going to have to spend the winter there, and the man decided to go into town to get the things they would need: flour and salt and coffee. And I guess they figured they'd spend the winter in the dugout. The woman was expecting a child, so she didn't go with him. Well a blizzard came while he was gone and he couldn't get back for eight days. When he finally was able to get back, he went into the dugout. The wind was blowing in through the blanket and his wife was dead on the floor. Cold. But the new baby was there—crying. It had been born while he was gone. He covered his wife, though she was dead and cold already, and picked up the baby and wrapped it up. And then he went through the snow—it was still snowing—about three miles to the next farm, where there was a woman, and he gave the baby to her. And, you know, that woman nursed the baby and... she raised that baby up and she grew up to be one of the prettiest young women in the county.

Anna Johnson, a Swedish American, feeds the chickens on her farm near Jamestown, New York, around 1910. Many Swedish immigrants settled in Jamestown.

Icelander Ogh Magnusson cares for her sheep in Washington. Raising sheep was popular in the Icelandic American community because it had been a major part of life in Iceland. Natural wools of gray, black, and brown were combined in traditional patterns for clothing.

FACTORIES AND UNIONS

Swedish workers inside the factory of the J. P. Danielson Company make small machine parts. The machine-tool company in Jamestown, New York, was founded by John Peter Danielson in partnership with Karl Peterson in 1902.

The employees of Lindeke Roller Mills, many of them Scandinavian, at their plant in St. Paul, Minnestoa, around 1900. The flour mills processed the grain produced by the surrounding farms.

Hans Jacobsen immigrated to the United States from Denmark in 1893. Two years later he wrote a letter describing his work in Swift's Meat Packing House in Chicago.

I have now worked for this Co. for about 14 days. The work does not much appeal to me, that is to say, it does not appeal at all. I work the whole time in a cold storage room, a big room with no windows and only a few electric lights. The temperature is kept at freezing, or perhaps a degree and a half above, year round. I handle about 10,000 pounds of sausages a day. As soon as they are made in an adjoining room, the sausages are hung on rods with about 40 pounds per rod. When the small carts bring them in to us, I have to take them and hang them in rows. One row is about as high as my chest, so that is easy enough, but the second is exactly as high as I can reach. In the long run, it is very strenuous work to hang up sausages.... In addition, I have to pack the sausages that are ready. There are two of us in the cold storage room. The other man is an old German who has worked here for nine years. Of course, he lets me do all the unpleasant work, and you really cannot blame him. When we are very busy, we get half a dozen young girls to help us pack the small packages. In addition to the sausages, we have sausage meat to take care of, but since we do not pack more than about 500 pounds of that a day, it is not of so much importance.

We work from 7 in the morning to 5:30 in the afternoon with half an hour for lunch.... Most of the workers in the department where I work are Germans with a small minority of Irishmen.... There are several policemen around the place who make sure that no one steals anything.

Atterdag Wermelin helped organize the socialist movement in Sweden in the 1880s. He left for the United States in 1887. Eight years later, he wrote to a friend in Sweden describing the work he found.

The most devilish job I have had was at a steel or rolling mill in Pueblo, Colorado. I worked from seven in the morning to six in the evening and three days a week I was forced to come back at seven in the evening and work until twelve midnight; indeed it happened at least a couple of times that I worked until three [A.M.], and then came back and began again at seven in the morning. What do you say about that? What do you say about the fact that my foreman could come to me on such occasions and say—as through it were a great favor—that now I could go home and go to bed? I have worked at that damned hellhole, the steel mill in Pueblo—four different times. The last time it was worse than ever before—worse than

anyone can imagine, who has not experienced it. The business did have one bright side to it. I made good money, as much as 100 dollars a month. When I came here I had 140 dollars in debts, when I left I had 150 dollars in savings pretty nearly.

In 1905, Karl-Johan Ellington, a Swedish immigrant, wrote critically of working conditions in the United States. He described his job at an organ factory in Moline, Illinois.

I began work at the organ factory. This was owned by a couple of Swedes who had "gotten ahead" and was to be sure no health resort. The first winter was unbearable. My small, private workroom was supposed to be warmed by a little stove. There were cracks in the floor and under it was some kind of storeroom where it was just as cold as it was outside. The following winters were even more unbearable, for the whole floor was converted into a single large room, and so that the [employers] might save storage space around the walls, they committed the unheard-of stupidity of placing the long-awaited pipes for the steam heating up on the ceiling! Here one had to stand with the steam heat overhead and the icy draft from the cracks in the floor and from a gaping elevator shaft. The whole thing was a special experimental laboratory for investigating just how much an organ builder can physically take. To be afflicted with colds was naturally one's "normal" condition, but in addition, I picked up...a thorough dose of rheumatism.... Besides, the steam heat was not there for the workers' sake but for the sake of the material. Ugh! And what was more, I was forced to stay where I was, whether they piled up ice or steam pipes around me, for they knew very well that I had my sick sister to take care of and pay living and medical expenses for.

These Danes work in a tailor shop in Racine, Wisconsin. Almost one-half of Racine's population was of Danish descent, making it "the most Danish city in the United States," as it was generally known.

The Bisbee Deportation

On June 27, 1917, a strike began among mine workers in Bisbee, Arizona. Less than three months earlier, the United States had entered World War I. Because the strike halted production at the region's copper mines, it was regarded as a threat to the U.S. war effort. The International Workers of the World (IWW), which had many Finnish American members, had helped organize the strike. Newspapers claimed that members of the IWW were disloyal to the United States.

The sheriff of the county secretly organized a "vigilance committee" to break the strike. On July 12, about 2,000 armed vigilantes marched to the homes of the striking workers and others suspected of being sympathetic to the strike.

Matt Hanhila, the young son of one of the Finnish American strikers, recalled the event:

"We were wakened that morning by a loud knock at the door. My bed was in the living room, and I was there when my father got up to go to the front door.... Silhouetted against the sky I could see several men on our porch, armed with rifles. They had come for my father....

"I do not recall what was said, but I do recall seeing my father let his eyes stray to the top of the boxed door frame over which he had his 32 automatic. I can remember, too, with a little feeling of guilt, that I wanted him to take his automatic and fight it out western style.

"Finally, after a short period of contemplation, my father decided to bow to the odds, and he went, although reluctantly, with the deputies of the vigilance committee. They took him without hat or coat to the pre-arranged gathering place...whence they were marched to the baseball field in Warren, three miles away, where they were all corralled."

About 1,200 men were forced onto railroad cattle cars at gunpoint and taken to a detention camp in Columbus, New Mexico. Matt Hanhila's mother was forced to sell the family home. She and Matt joined his father in Columbus, where they lived in a tent. The strikers were held for weeks or months without trials. Finally they were released but were prevented from returning to Bisbee.

Workers forced onto the railroad track at gunpoint.

John Anderson, born in 1906, was the grandson of Norwegian immigrants. He grew up on a farm about 200 miles northwest of Milwaukee, Wisconsin. He described his early factory jobs.

As soon as I graduated from high school I bought a train ticket for Milwaukee. With no previous experience and no one to advise me. I went from factory to factory asking for any job that was listed on bulletin boards at the employment offices. After two or three days of job hunting I was hired at A. O. Smith, a large employer making seamless tubing for the petroleum industry and car frames for General Motors cars. A. O. Smith was an anti-union company that checked the record of its new hires for union activity. My coming from a farm was assurance enough that I had no union ideas.

When I first went to work assembling frames by hand it took four or five men to assemble each frame. The parts for the frame were not only oily and dirty but they had sharp edges on which one could be seriously cut. The air was filled with smoke and dirt. At the end of a twelve hour day I would be completely exhausted....

When my roommate got a job metal finishing at Seaman Body I decided to follow him there in January 1926. It took me about a month to learn the metal finishing operation. We used a soldering iron, several heavy files, finishing hammers, and emery cloth. It required skill to use a soldering iron so that a minimum of finishing was needed; then one had to learn how to use a file to make the solder and metal perfectly smooth. The more skill one had the easier the work was. It was necessary to wear canvas gloves, not only to protect the hands but also to feel the smoothness of the metal. We wore out a pair of these gloves every day or so and we had to buy our own gloves.

In 1889, 16-year-old Mary Anderson came to the United States from Sweden. Settling in Michigan, she first worked as a housekeeper in a boardinghouse for lumberjacks. After starting to work in a shoe factory in Chicago, she joined a union. Later she was an organizer for the union and in 1919 became head of the newly created Women's Bureau of the U.S. Department of Labor. In her autobiography, she described her job stitching shoes in a factory.

I never got bored with that job because fitting the lining [of the shoe] to the outside and stitching it had to be done carefully or else the next process, "vamping," could not be done. I always look back on my life in that factory, where six or seven hundred people worked, as very interesting because this was my first factory experience and I learned that factory life is not just the work at a machine. You make contacts with other people.... I didn't know what a union was, but I was ready to join because I wanted to be with others and do what they are doing, and that is what I thought the union meant.

In the 1930s, the right to organize unions was guaranteed by federal law. Reino Hannula, the son of Finnish immigrants, described the climax of a strike in Gardner, Massachusetts, against the O. W. Siebert Company in 1935. The workers demanded recognition of

Bitter feelings split the Finnish community in Michigan's Upper Peninsula during a strike in the copper mines in 1913–14. Dressed in their Sunday best, union workers carry a sign (only partially visible in this photo) that reads, "Scab women leading scab to work." Before the strike ended in defeat for the union, men had been killed on both sides. The children were also partisans, with scuffles between the two sides leading to black eyes like the one on the boy at center front.

the United Furniture and Allied Trade Workers union and a five-cents-an-hour raise. However, a local judge had issued an injunction against picketing by the strikers.

Axel Bachman [the union president] carefully explained the "pickle" the union was in. The injunction, he insisted, was not fair but, even so, those who defied it were liable to go to jail. Every union official, he added, was willing to defy the injunction because there was no reasonable alternative....

My brother Toivo, treasurer of the union, jumped up on the secretary's table and yelled as loud as he could, "I move that the United Furniture and Allied Trade Workers declare a general strike in support of the O. W. Siebert strikers! All union members will be on the picket line tomorrow!"

The motion was never seconded. A tremendous roar sounded...throughout the hall as the workers yelled their acclamation. Several union members jumped on the table and shouted, "General strike tomorrow! General strike tomorrow!"

The words "General strike" echoed through the building and into the street. The workers of Gardner were venting their anger against the injunction and the judge.

The next day the factory workers in Gardner responded to the union's general strike call in numbers far beyond anyone's expectation. They left their jobs and marched, usually in a group, to the O. W. Siebert factory. The union officers were amazed as group after group of marching workers joined the picket line....

The continuous circle of defiant pickets were in extremely high spirits. They sang, shouted, and joked as they walked around and around the city block....

A few days later the O. W. Siebert Company agreed to a 5¢ per hour wage increase and to recognize the United Furniture and Allied Trade Workers as the sole bargaining agent for its employees. The union had passed its first big test. It was in Gardner to stay.

Legendary Swedish American labor organizer Joe Hill (born Joel Hägglund in Sweden) wrote many of the songs in the Little Red Song Book of the International Workers of the World. The Rebel Girl was one.

The toboggan slide at Taylors Falls, Minnesota, around 1888. Coming from northern Europe, all Scandinavian immigrant groups enjoyed winter sports as part of community life.

CHAPTER FIVE

PUTTING DOWN ROOTS

**W**e have it good, *but America is not Norway,*" one immigrant declared. "There is always something strange and unfamiliar about everything here." To feel more secure in their new land, Scandinavians—like other immigrants— formed their own communities and neighborhoods.

Laurence M. Larson was two years old when his family immigrated in 1870. He later wrote about the Norwegian American community in Forest City, Iowa, where they settled.

"We lived as Norwegians, or as nearly so as conditions would permit.... English was recognized as the language of the land and was acknowledged to be of first importance. Adult immigrants were not, however, so very keen about learning to speak or write this language.... There was, for that matter, only small incentive to learn [English]. Nearly all our business transactions could be (and frequently were) carried out in Norwegian."

In the mid-19th century, similar Norwegian American communities spread from Illinois to the Dakotas. In the words of historian Oscar Handlin, they formed "a nation within a nation...loyal to one another and with a commitment to the United States and its principles."

In 1910, 57.3 percent of the Norwegian-born people in the U.S. lived in three states: Wisconsin, Minnesota, and North Dakota. Seattle, Washington, and the borough of Brooklyn, New York, also had high percentages of Norwegian Americans. In 1920, Brooklyn had the largest Norwegian urban population outside Norway itself.

The first Swedes in Chicago arrived in the 1830s, when Fort Dearborn, the city's first structure, was still standing. During the next 70 years, Chicago had the second-largest Swedish population of any city in the world. In 1900, about 150,000 Swedish Americans lived there, most in a neighborhood known as Andersonville, around Clark and Foster Avenues.

In 1890, the Swedish American journalist Isador Kjellberg wrote, "The liveliest section of the busy Chicago Avenue shows, its entire length, a large mass of exclusively Swedish signs, that Anderson, Petterson, and Lundstrom were here conducting a Swedish general store, a Swedish bookshop, a Swedish beer saloon...and so on. And wherever one goes one hears Swedish sounds generally, and if one's thoughts are somewhat occupied, one can believe one has been quickly transported back to Sweden."

Chicago had 61 Swedish Lutheran churches by 1924. They were centers of community life. Each Sunday many of the churches served herring breakfasts.

Many Danes also settled in Chicago. By 1920, there were three distinct Danish neighborhoods in the city. Until the 1930s, Chicago had the largest urban population of Danes outside of Denmark itself. Indeed, more than any other Scandinavian group, Danes tended to settle in cities. By 1970, only 4 percent of Danish Americans lived in rural areas. Today, the two cities with the largest Danish American populations are Chicago and Los Angeles.

Many different Scandinavian groups lived in Brooklyn, New York. Bay Ridge, one section of Brooklyn, became a Little Scandinavia. Shops sold products from Norway and Sweden. Popular foods included Norwegian *lefse athin* (flat bread made from potatoes) and Swedish *limpa* (bread flavored with anise and molasses). Church suppers served crayfish, *lutefisk* (fish preserved in lye), and *gravlax* (salmon cured in sugar, salt, white pepper, and dill). The saloons sold *aquavit,* a caraway-flavored drink made from fermented potatoes. Many clubs, lodges, and charitable organizations sprang up, along with Scandinavian American hospitals, schools, and an orphanage.

In 1912, New York's Swedish community staged a grand parade to celebrate the Swedish victories in the 1912 Stockholm Olympics. Members of many associations and organizations marched, wearing blue-and-yellow sashes (the colors of the Swedish flag) and the folk costumes of their native land.

Almost all Finnish immigrants chose to settle in the 13 states along the northern border of the United States. In 1900, almost half of all the Finnish-born citizens of the United States lived in Michigan and Minnesota. However, New York, Massachusetts, and Maine also had sizable numbers of Finns.

Fitchburg, Massachusetts, was a typical community. Its people were divided into Church Finns and Hall Finns. Church Finns were religious and politically conservative. Hall Finns were militant socialists and members of the labor movement. Here too, as in many other Finnish American communities, a temperance society discouraged the use of alcoholic beverages.

In 1900, the three Finnish American groups in Fitchburg joined forces. The reason was simple economics: they needed to pool their resources to build a meeting place. The result was the Messiah Lutheran Church. Five years later, however, the labor-oriented Saima Society built its own hall.

Finn halls like Fitchburg's were the center of most Finnish American communities. The first generation of immigrants built an estimated 500 Finn halls. They served as meeting places, but perhaps more impor-tantly, almost all contained a theater.

Theater groups were immensely popular among the Finnish Americans. Men who worked all day in factories or mines and women who worked as maids, seamstresses, and laundresses all showed up in the evening to rehearse that week's play.

Finn halls also sponsored such cultural and social groups as brass bands, singing groups, and women's sewing circles. One Finn hall, in the town of Virginia, Minnesota, had an opera house. There was a Finn hall on Fifth Avenue in New York City's Harlem section, where

A reunion of the Juntunen family at their farmhouse in Esko, Minnesota, on Christmas Eve, 1932. Some of the family members sit on rag rugs made from old clothes that were cut into strips and woven together.

many Finns lived in the early 20th century.

Close to each Finn hall, and sometimes part of it, was a sauna, the traditional Finnish steam bath. On Saturday nights, virtually everyone spent an hour or so in the sauna house. It was a time for socializing and discarding everyday cares and concerns. Most of the close-knit Finnish American communities also sponsored a cooperative store that sold goods to its members at low prices.

Mayme Westervik Lumppio, the daughter of Finnish immigrants, grew up in Cloquet, Minnesota, in the 1920s. She recalled: "The Co-op Store and the Finn Hall played a big part in the early years. The clerks in the store all spoke Finnish, and all the doings at the hall were in the Finnish language. My family did not miss anything there. The plays were great, as were the programs, dances, and weddings."

Icelandic Americans who came to Utah because they were Mormons lived around the town of Spanish Fork. The majority of Icelandic immigrants settled in North Dakota and Minnesota. Some also put down roots on the West Coast and in the cities where other Scandinavian Americans lived.

In the rural areas, Icelandic Americans formed close communities. The Lutheran church was the focus of social activities. Choirs and bands performed both classical European and Icelandic music.

Icelanders—both in Iceland and the United States—had a high degree of literacy. Reading aloud from Icelandic classics and newspapers was a favorite family pastime. Many Icelandic American communities organized reading circles that purchased books in Icelandic that members shared and discussed.

All the Scandinavian American groups published newspapers in their native languages. These kept the immigrants aware of events in their homelands, but they also carried news of the far-flung Scandinavian communities in the United States. Thus, these ethnic newspapers became a force that united the relatively small populations of Scandinavian Americans.

Like all other immigrant groups, the Scandinavian Americans formed many clubs and organizations. Some provided unemployment benefits and insurance for their members. Others were dedicated to preserving the culture and traditions of their native lands.

A Swedish Society was founded in New York City in 1836. Chicago's Swedes formed a Svea Society in 1857. Chicago was also the headquarters of the Order of Svithiod and the Viking Order, founded later in the 19th century. Today, the largest Swedish American organization is the Vasa Order of America, founded in New Haven, Connecticut, in 1896. By 1928 it had 400 lodges throughout the United States.

Norwegian American associations often presented dramatic or musical performances, carrying on Norwegian traditions. Many Norwegian American communities had *bygdelags*, clubs whose members (or their ancestors) came from the same *bygd*, or region, in Norway. Members of the *bygdelags* usually gathered in midsummer. Wearing traditional costumes, they danced to and sang the music of their native Norway.

The Sons of Norway, founded in 1895 in Minneapolis, became the major national Norwegian American group. It is a mutual aid society, a social club, and an organization that promotes Norwegian cultural traditions.

For similar reasons, Danish Americans joined the Danish Brotherhood and, in the Far West (Cali-

fornia, Washington, and Oregon), Dania. The major Finnish American group was the Finnish Brotherhood, or Knights of Kaleva, named in honor of the Finnish national epic, the *Kalevala*. In 1919, the Icelandic National League was founded to keep alive Icelandic culture in American communities. All these groups had corresponding women's auxiliaries and organizations.

Temperance societies, formed to discourage the use of alcoholic beverages, were very active in Scandinavian American communities. Some

Choral singing was a great favorite of Scandinavians, and groups often gathered to compete. The Norwegian Singers Association of America held this Sangerfest in Fargo, North Dakota, in 1912.

temperance groups sponsored performances of music, art, and theater.

The great majority of Scandinavian immigrants were Lutherans. In the United States, various Lutheran synods, or associated church councils, were formed. Swedish American and Norwegian American Lutherans formed the Augustana Synod in 1860. The Norwegians soon split off to form their own synod, which became closely allied with the German-origin Missouri Synod.

The Icelandic Lutheran Synod was organized in 1884. It became

the most important unifying force among Icelandic Americans. In turn, Finnish Lutherans formed the Suomi Synod. (*Suomi* is the Finnish word for Finland.)

Danish Lutheran churches in the United States reflected the divisions between Lutherans in Denmark. The two major church branches in the United States were known as the Inner Mission and the Grundtvigian (named after Danish theologian and poet Nikolai Grundtvig). More familiarly, the members of each group were known, respectively, as "the holy Danes" or "the happy Danes."

Grundtvigians organized unique institutions known as folk schools. In addition to the usual academic subjects, the Danish American folk schools taught Danish church history, mythology, and cultural practices such as folk dancing. Between 1878 and 1911, five folk schools were founded in Iowa, Michigan, Nebraska, Minnesota, and California. Danish Americans throughout the United States financially supported the folk schools and sent their children to them.

Scandinavian Americans also founded colleges to preserve their cultural and religious traditions. These include Augustana College in Sioux Falls, South Dakota (founded in 1860); Augustana College in Rock Island, Illinois (1860); Luther College in Decorah, Iowa (1861); Gustavus Adolphus College in St. Peter, Minnesota (1862); St. Olaf's College in Northfield, Minnesota (1874); Dana College in Blair, Nebraska (1884); Grand View College in Des Moines, Iowa (1896); and Suomi College in Hancock, Michigan (1904).

Icelandic women socialize as they work in North Dakota. One of the women demonstrates how to spin wool using the distinctive Icelandic spinning wheel; another cards wool. North Dakota had more Icelandic immigrants than any other state.

COMMUNITIES

The Raaen family lived in a Norwegian American settlement in the Dakota Territory in the late 1800s. The youngest daughter, Kjersti, kept a diary in which she described the New Year's festivities.

Last night was New Year's Eve, and we went Christmas mumming. No, you can't go on Christmas Eve, because that is Christ's birthday, but you can begin in the evening on Christmas Day and keep on every evening till New Year's Eve. The neighbor's children came; so there were six of us, all dressed as crazily as possible so that no one would know us. Aagot [her older sister] dressed Tosten [her brother] and me. She put a long white dress of her own on him and tied a cord around his waist. She made a mask out of part of a flour sack—I wonder what Mor [mother] will say when she sees that a flour sack has been cut up. Such a looking mask! There were holes for the eyes and nose, charcoal marks for eyebrows, and a stiff paper rolled to look like a long nose. She cut an opening under the nose and sewed some red cloth on for lips; it was an awful-looking mouth, so crooked! After she put the mask on Tosten, she put Mor's old black hood on his head. Tosten was a witch.

She fixed me up so they would think I was a boy dressed like a girl. I had Far's [father's] old coat, cap, and mittens, Mor's old skirt, and Aagot's old shoes, so large they looked like boy's shoes. Aagot did not make me a pretty mask at all; she took flour sacking and cut openings for the eyes and nose and then put it on me. She tied a red kerchief on my head. It was good that we had so many clothes on outside our own, for it was a cold night.

We always have a good time at Even Midboe's so we decided to go there; he lives about a mile from us, but we didn't mind.... Before we knocked at the door, we decided that only Tosten should talk, because he can disguise his voice. Even must have heard something; he opened the door and saw us before we had a chance to knock. How his dark eyes twinkled, and he laughed so hard that he could hardly tell us to come in! It was so warm in his house that we thought we would melt. When the children saw Tosten they were scared and began to cry. Even talked to them, but I could see they were afraid anyway. He asked us where we came from and where we were going. Tosten said, "We come from east of the sun and west of the moon and we are going to a place where the sun never sets."...

Ingeborg, Even's wife, brought cookies, apples, and candy, and a glass of Christmas mead for each. We could not eat with our masks on; so we had to take them off. How surprised they were when they saw the witch was Tosten! The children all

Charles Samuelson stands in front of his store, Samuelson's Confectionery, in Minneapolis in 1890. Signs are in both Swedish and English.

came up to us and helped eat the nice things Ingeborg had put on the table.

Axel V. Swensson came to the United States from Sweden in 1911, when he was 20. After taking jobs in many places, he became manager of a J. C. Penney store in Decorah, Iowa. His daughter, Betty Swanson Cain, referred to him as "A. V." in her account of life there.

Decorah is a pretty town in the rolling hill country of northeastern Iowa.... Above our street there was a knoll called Pleasant Hill, where we kids used to ramble and sit on the grassy hillside stringing clover blossom necklaces, pushing dandelion stems into curls, and turning hollyhock flowers upside down to make dolls with wide skirts....

The population of Decorah was mostly Norwegian. A Swede, spelling his name with the tell-tale *-son* instead of the usual Norwegian *-sen*, coming in to manage a local business was a novelty. A. V., the lone Swede, exchanged good-natured ethnic jokes with the Norwegians. "How long do you think you're gonna last in this Norski town, A. V.?" "How can you trust a fellow who eats *Knäckebröd* (Swedish hardtack) instead of *lefse* (Norwegian flat, limp unleavened bread)?" Dad would answer, "Well, I see you Norskis are spending a lot of money in my store, so I must be doing O.K."

The Finn hall was the center of social life in Finnish American communities. Aarre Lahti recalled the activities at the Palace Finn Hall in Ironwood, Michigan.

Without assistance from financial institutions, these workers—using their own energy and determination—erected this huge hall with work bees (*talkoot*). The hall, after completion, boasted the best dance floor in the county and a stage with the necessary scenery, costumes, and mechanical equipment for a first class little theatre. And it was the only facility in town with gymnastic and "track" paraphernalia.

The hall was always "busy." In any given week, there were

Bay Ridge, a section of Brooklyn, New York, had a large Scandinavian community. These Swedish friends gathered for a neighborhood party in the 1910s.

Viola Turpeinen

In Finn Halls throughout the United States, people danced the polka and schottische to the music of the accordion. No performer was more popular in the Finnish American communities than Viola Turpeinen.

Viola Irene Turpeinen, the daughter of Walter and Signe Witala Turpeinen, was born in 1909 in Champion, Michigan. Both parents played the accordion, and Viola showed great talent for the instrument. She soon began entertaining at the local Finn Hall. A Finnish American musician, promoter, and comedian named John Rosendahl later heard her play and suggested that they combine their talents.

In 1927, they moved to New York City, which had, at the time, the nation's largest Finnish American population and was the center of the recording industry. With Rosendahl on violin and Turpeinen on accordion, the duo cut several records. In 1929, they toured Finland and were well received in Helsinki.

In 1933, Rosendahl died, ending the musical partnership. But a new musician, William Syrjälä, now became important in Turpeinen's life. Syrjälä played the violin, viola, guitar, and trumpet. He had first seen Turpeinen at a local hall in Cloquet, Minnesota, but they started performing together only after he arrived in New York.

A short time later they were married and went on tour to Finnish communities throughout the United States. Years later William Syrjälä claimed that he had been in more Finn Halls than any other person. Wherever they appeared, they drew large crowds of first- and second-generation Finns. Viola's nimble fingers flew across the keyboard and the liveliness of her music set everyone to dancing. In their first recording together, Viola sang a song composed by her husband and displayed a clear, pleasant voice. Her singing remained part of their act.

In 1952, the Syrjäläs moved to Lake Worth, Florida, where they built a home that Viola dubbed "The House that Polkas Built." She died in 1958, but the memory of her playing and her records set a very high standard for her successors. William Syrjälä continued entertaining at Lake Worth until his death in 1993.

band and orchestra practice sessions in addition to both men's and women's choir rehearsals. And the little theatre seemed to be always busy preparing productions involving drama or the opera. Of course, political meetings were held in the hall, too.

The athletic sessions were held on Tuesday and Thursday evenings and again on Sunday morning when the hall's auditorium was set up with parallel bars, a high bar, "horses," mats, and other gymnastic equipment. The weekday sessions began informally about five o'clock to accommodate those who were on the night shift.

Hop-skip-and-jump, the long jump, high jump, and the shotput were practiced. The discus-throwing was too erratic to be practiced there and the length of the property did not permit any javelin throwing either. Those who wanted to engage in those activities walked (or ran) to the Gogebic County Fairgrounds....

As the evening approached, the athletes would return to the hall where the orderly and regimented calisthenics (and drills with the heavy iron wands) would begin. The standing broad jump and the running broad jump were practiced in the basement of the hall. By eleven o'clock most members left, since their ten- or twelve-hour workday started at seven (or before) the next morning.

The sauna, or steam bath, was an important part of Finnish American life. In her autobiography My Story, Inkeri's Journey, *Inkeri Väänänen-Jensen, the daughter of Finnish immigrants, wrote about the sauna her family owned.*

Our public sauna in Virginia [Minnesota] covered almost our entire back lot. Since we did not have running hot water in the house, a huge boiler in the basement heated the water for the sauna and also heated the radiators in the sauna washrooms. The sauna bathers made steam by pulling on a rope attached to a water pipe with holes placed just above the radiator, thus releasing a water spray over the hot radiator, creating steam. At the back of the sauna building was a large dressing room for men and boys adjoining a large room with stools, pails, and soap for washing up. This in turn led into a steam room with long bleachers and cedar *vihtas* (switches), plus pails and soap. For families and women alone, there were two steam rooms, one on each side of the long hall leading to the men's section. There was a dressing room at each end of these two steam rooms, making a total of four private dressing rooms. When one group finished using the steam room and had retreated to the dressing room, the steam room was cleaned up, and new bathers were ushered into the other dressing room....

In the waiting room, with its wooden benches around the walls for those who had to wait their turn, Irma [her sister] handed out towels, took the money, made change, escorted the family groups into the dressing rooms, and sold the pop that was cooling on ice in a round metal washtub on the waiting room floor. The cost for a sauna was twenty-five cents for an adult; this included a large towel. Maybe children were free or,

A chorus of singers forms the Norwegian flag at the fairgrounds in Minneapolis in celebration of the centennial of Norwegian immigration in June 1925.

at the most, ten cents.... Some people carried a cloth sauna bag with their own towels, washcloths, clean clothes, or whatever they needed.

Maren Lorensen, who had worked as a hired girl on a Danish farm, arrived in Racine, Wisconsin, in 1893. She described her experiences in letters to a friend.

Y ou should really be here, you would never regret it. That is if you do not suffer from homesickness, because then it can be very bad to be so far away as it is not easy to run home to mother.... I cannot remember if I have told you that sister Marie has gotten married—that was at Christmas—to a fellow from the town nearest Svenstrup. He has been over here for seven years and has even earned some money. They live in a fine home; they have carpets on all the floors. There are long white curtains, a sofa and a rocking chair, paintings, big mirrors, a treadle sewing machine, and many, many things I cannot describe. They live much better over here than at home. They get fine cakes at every meal....

Most of the houses here are built of wood, but many are built and painted so beautifully. They are not built so close together as in the towns at home. The streets are not cobbled in many places, and the sidewalks are all of boards, but otherwise it looks very much like back home....

W e are all having such a good time over here; we do not miss Denmark at all as there are enough Danes here. We get together and have a good time, with dancing and fun as at home. It would be nice to be able to run home once in a while and talk to family and old friends, but that is not possible, and we have to live without it. People are not nearly so high and mighty here as back home.

Jon Halldorsson came to the United States from Iceland in 1872. He settled in Milwaukee with a few other Icelanders. In his first letter home he described how they pooled their resources to make ends meet.

I am never lonesome, have plenty to do in my spare time. Ten hours work a day does not seem much to one who is accustomed to work sixteen. This is the country for unmarried men, who have no special ties, or young married ones with

The postmaster and mail carriers of Norse, Texas, in front of the first post office in this Norwegian American town. It also served as a general store.

one child.... Six of us Icelanders have started a cooperative household, now a week old. The rent for three rooms is five dollars a month. We each contributed seven dollars and bought a stove, beds, chairs, table, and dishes. It is surprising how much we could buy for that amount of money. We bought our things and moved in after five o'clock last Saturday.

Many Swedes settled in Minneapolis in the late 19th century. A Swedish immigrant living there wrote to his brother in Sweden in 1897.

I am not out much for entertainment but if there is some good Swedish affair I am there in a corner. We have Swedish theater sometimes and parties of different kinds which are quite nice. The other day we had a rousing surprise party in honor of Mr. and Mrs. Nils Ringlund. There was a great feed and Ringlund got from us one hundred fifty or so friends a remembrance worth around one hundred dollars, which says incidentally, "He is honored who deserves to be honored." Ringlund and wife are among the best people you could hope to meet.

Marie Torheim Berglund left Norway in 1911 and settled in Canada. Three years later she moved to Tacoma, Washington. She wrote about the Norwegian community there.

In 1914, I came down to Tacoma. My friend Kristina...was working in a cafe here and there was a place [job] vacant. This restaurant, we called it coffee house, that was Henry's place, 1305 Commerce Street [she later married Henry Berglund]. There was so many Norwegians there that you could talk Norwegian all day long. Mostly men; now and then a woman would come, but very seldom. In the morning they would serve oatmeal mush, with the milk and sugar and coffee. And they had such good ham sandwiches....

As young people in the Good Templar Lodge, we had really good entertainment. We had singing, we had folk dances, we had debating, and we had somebody writing a paper on a certain subject. It was about things going on and what we remem-

The whole town of Decorah, Iowa, turned out for a parade on Water Street in 1909. Decorah was another midwestern town with strong Norwegian roots.

Cooperative stores were an important social center in most Finnish communities. The members of this co-op line up in their store in Sebaka, Minnesota, in 1939.

ber about home and what we should do here.... We were all Norwegians, nothing but Norwegians....

The Daughters of Norway started 1907 [in Tacoma]. The Sons had already started.... At Normanna Hall, we Daughters met in the small hall and the Sons met in the big hall.... I was on the first bazaar committee.... It lasted three days between Christmas and New Year, when all these loggers came in. It was stormy and rainy and we did not even have doors into the hall; they had just some boards to keep the rain out. We done tremendous well.

At one time, the Daughters were close to four hundred members. We have a kind of feeling of the same background, that interest in keeping cultural things alive. Something to live for, to take pride in.

Chicago was a magnet for many Scandinavians and became the largest Swedish American community in the United States. Anders Larsson, who emigrated in 1846, became a leader of the city's Svea Society. He wrote a letter in 1876 in which he described the society's efforts to unite Chicago's Swedes.

Temperance societies attacked the drinking problems sometimes found in Scandinavian communities. These Swedish American women demonstrate their opinions on a parade float in Worcester, Massachusetts, around 1915.

Now I should say something about America and the Swedes here, who in Chicago alone are around eighteen thousand, but strangely enough they have altogether too much of the hereditary sin, or in other words the Royal Swedish Jealousy. All the other nationalities, meanwhile, are, as the old saying goes, like peas in a pod. But all the attempts that have been made and are being made among us sooner or later go on the rocks. The Svea Society has nevertheless been doing its best for twenty years now, though often amid storms and winter winds. Dozens of Swedish societies under a variety of different names have been born and have died unmissed by the survivors; the reason must in some part be that Svea has a good library. Before the fire [that devastated Chicago in 1871] we had over two thousand books, all of which disappeared within a few minutes, but now we already have not quite eight hundred. I have been the librarian for eight years and this is now actually my only occupation and amusement, which from my childhood has also been my greatest pleasure. We are now awaiting more books from Sweden and there are beginning to be plenty of Swedish books here, though they are expensive. There are many booksellers and lending libraries, beside the excellent Chicago library...also newspapers in all languages. In Swedish there are 1,500 volumes and two newspapers.

The Big Store in Minneota, Minnesota, advertised "Fancy Patent Flour" during the 1909 Fourth of July parade. Started by Icelander Olafur G. Anderson, the store served a large area around the community.

Julius Petersen, a Danish immigrant, wrote his brother in Denmark to describe Chicago's festivities on the Fourth of July, 1887.

Yesterday Rasmus and Marine were finally married. Their wedding was a crowning touch to the Fourth of July. Already by the middle of last week boys began to shoot fireworks on the streets. All of the shops were full of flags ranging in size from five by eight centimeters to four by six meters. It became worse and worse every day, and on Sunday there was a lot of noise. But Monday, 4 July was a bright day, a grand day

Carl Sandburg

Carl Sandburg, the son of Swedish immigrants, became one of the most widely read American poets of the 20th century. He also won the Pulitzer Prize in history in 1940 for his biography of Abraham Lincoln.

Sandburg was born in 1878 in Galesburg, Illinois. His father, August, was a railroad worker and blacksmith who could barely write his name. Young Carl took a series of jobs such as dishwasher, milk-wagon driver, bootblack, farmer, and barber—anything to help him get by. These years gave him a sympathy for working people that he would never lose.

In 1898, with the outbreak of the Spanish-American War, Sandburg enlisted as a soldier. Afterward, he decided to get an education and enrolled in Lombard College in Galesburg. After graduation, he found a job writing for the *Chicago Daily News,* and he worked in the newspaper's Stockholm bureau in 1918.

Three years earlier, he had published his first book of poetry, *Chicago Poems.* Although some critics praised his work, others were shocked. Sandburg used everyday speech and even slang to celebrate the laborers and working-class life of Chicago. His later works included a children's book, *Rootabaga Stories* (1922), and collections of folk songs. Sandburg loved to perform these songs in public, accompanying himself on the guitar or the mandolin.

His biography of Abraham Lincoln was the product of 20 years of research and writing. *The Prairie Years*, the first part of the multivolume biography, was published in 1926, followed in 1939 by *The War Years.* Sandburg strongly identified with Lincoln. He had grown up in the same area where the martyred president had lived. Sandburg emphasized the human drama of Lincoln's Presidency and the agony of making decisions with life-or-death consequences.

During World War II, Sandburg gave lectures on the evils of Nazism and the importance of the Allied cause. In the postwar years, he became a widely admired radio commentator and newspaper columnist. He won a second Pulitzer Prize for his collected poetry in 1951. When he died in 1967, he was one of the most respected and beloved American writers.

for many, especially Rasmus. I almost thought the world was coming to an end (joke), because beginning at 4 a.m. I could hardly hear myself speak because of the noise. The houses were almost completely hidden by the flags, and were literally shaking from the cannon volleys. Many windows were broken. There were flags of every imaginable kind. Of course, 90 percent of them were the Stars and Stripes, but there were several Danish flags and many Norwegian and Swedish ones. In the morning seventeen Scandinavian societies marched in a parade here on the West Side. The first one was the "Danish Veterans of Chicago," about one-hundred fifty strong, all wearing memorial medals. Street urchins had literally filled the streetcar tracks with firecrackers, so there was a constant cracking under the wheels.

The Danish church where Rasmus and Marine were married is in a very quiet street, so fortunately there was some peace and quiet outside her aunt's house, where we were served wine and cake. We male guests drank a lot of it in honor of them. The bride and groom changed clothes and we followed them on the streetcar down to the Racine steamer, which they boarded at 8 p.m. for their honeymoon trip. Here in America it is customary for a bride and groom to begin their wedding trip the same evening they are married. All steamships and trains have so-called "bridal chambers."

When we came back home from Lake Michigan the fireworks had begun in earnest. Firecrackers were thrown into the streetcar where we sat, and salvos were fired right in front of the horse's noses. They didn't know what was happening, of course. The poor motorman had to stand with his hand on the brake all the time in order to stop whenever the horses were frightened. Several times they nearly turned over the streetcar. Finally we arrived home.

Right next to where we live there are fire and police stations, and fireworks worth eight hundred dollars were to be set off. We arrived just in time to see it. Two balloons went up, and enormous number of rockets, golden dragons, and flaming wheels exploded. The remarkable thing is that people stood right next to where the fireworks were ignited, so some received small burns and many had holes burned in their clothing. We stood way over on the other side of the street, but nevertheless Juul's daughter, who had come to the wedding with us, had her new dress destroyed. A rocket came right at us and hit her. Those of us who stood next to her helped brush the sparks off, but they burned several large holes in the dress, so it was completely ruined. She had paid fourteen dollars for it eight days ago.

Bergljot Anker Nilssen was born in Norway in 1891. After her friend Karl Nilssen returned from the United States in 1915, they were married. Karl left for Chicago in 1922, and after he found a job, Bergljot and their young son Jens joined him. In 1928 she wrote to Karl's parents and sister in Norway.

Yesterday Jens and I went and saw the Norwegian film that the Norwegian America Line has been showing in many cities here in this country. We saw cities and towns all over Norway. Krogh sang—over here they say he is

Norway's best singer, but I don't believe that can be true. His voice is nothing compared to the voices I have heard in the opera here. Neib from Tistedalen played the violin. The hall was filled, and it was interesting to hear people speaking Norwegian with English words mixed in. There were people there who had been in this country for thirty or forty years, and it was moving to hear their comments when pictures from their home areas were shown. Jens was enthusiastic about the sports at home, and he asked, "Why can't we go to Norway for a few years?" But you can't live off the beautiful country, so he wouldn't have what he has here. Three Norwegian children's homes and two Norwegian old folks' homes have been invited to the performances. There will be six showings in Chicago—and all will surely be to a full house.

In 1993, Bob Arnesen, a social studies teacher, remembered growing up in the Scandinavian American neighborhood of Bay Ridge, Brooklyn, New York, in the 1940s and 1950s.

Eighth Avenue in Bay Ridge was called Lopskaus Boulevard, after the Scandinavian stew into which all the leftovers are thrown. It was the shopping area for Finntown, which was on Eighth Avenue around the Forties, and the Scandinavian community.

The stores were reminiscent of Europe. People shopped every day for fresh food. Bay Ridge was a mixed neighborhood. There were Scandinavian bakeries, delicatessens, and fish stores, but the candy stores were mostly owned by Jews, the ice-cream parlors by Germans, the fruit stores by Italians, the bars and grills by Irish. It was an island of small stores....

When my grandfather came to live with us, he spent his days in the bars and grills of Bay Ridge, where he drank his schnapps and enjoyed the camaraderie. The bars were something like the English pubs, gathering places for primarily Irish and Scandinavian men....

From Sixty-ninth street up, the Brooklyn waterfront was lined with docks, which probably is why so many Scandinavians settled in Bay Ridge. They were seafaring people, and many worked on the ships.

Eleanor Bystrom Law, the daughter of Swedish immigrants, had her own memories of Bay Ridge as it was in the 1920s and 1930s.

Well, it was very, very nice. It had a lot of people from one place, that is Swedes from Sweden and Norwegians from Norway. We had Swedish delicatessens, bakeries, grocery stores. They sold herring and *sylte* [head cheese]. My mother made her own sausages and breads. Saturday was baking day. She made *bullas*, which are rolls that you cut from a loaf, like bread, flavored with cardamom.

We children did a lot of roller skating, played tag on the streets. That was the only place to play. We played ring-a-levio, jumped rope. We didn't ski, because you had to have a car. I went ice skating a few times. Up till I started to play on the street, I spoke Swedish at home. Then the other kids looked at

Boardinghouses provided shelter and the kinds of food immigrants wanted. The boarders and staff of the Elanto Cooperative Boarding House in Nashwauk, Minnesota, were primarily Finnish.

Skiing was a popular sport in the countries of Scandinavia, and immigrants brought their love of it with them to the United States. This ski jump competition took place in Duluth, Minnesota, in 1910.

Drama was part of the Scandinavian American cultural scene, and Finns, in particular, developed a passion for staging plays. Sometimes, the whole community participated in the productions. The Edith Koivisto Touring Company staged a Finnish production of Carmen *in Marquette, Michigan, around 1926.*

you and said, "Well, why don't you speak English?" I guess I learned English on the street.

In downtown Brooklyn, there was the Swedish American Athletic Club. The fellows would go down there and play pool. What else did they do? They had dances. That was what kept the place going. Regular dances, waltzes, fox trots, schottisches and hambos and all those dances.

Jim Jensen, a former television newscaster in New York City, recalled his boyhood in Kenosha, Wisconsin. His father arrived in 1919 and settled in Kenosha, where he worked as a machinist and married a German American woman.

We had wonderful food. Pork roast, sausages, goose, duck, along with lingonberries and certain kinds of berries from Iceland and Greenland. There were two Danish bakeries in Kenosha when I was a kid. Norgaard's and Nilssen's. My father knew them both very well. I can remember going into the back room to see the great big machines that mixed the dough. For coffee cakes, cookies....

My father belonged to a lodge, the Danish Brotherhood. Everybody paid dues, and out of that came health benefits and unemployment insurance for the members. They brought that idea from Europe, where many of them were socialists. Of course there were parties and dances at the Danish Brotherhood's hall. At Christmas the Danish Brotherhood set up a tree 25 or 30 feet high. They had an orchestra and dancing, gave the kids candy canes and toys. It was a blast!

Each of the ethnic groups in town had its own similar organization and hall. The Germans, the Italians, the Slovaks. Each group had its own lodge and hall. It wasn't as if they were hostile to each other. On the contrary. But they liked to gather with others with similar traditions, spoke the same language. If you went to the Danish Brotherhood, you spoke Danish. At church, the services, the sermon, my confirmation ceremony—all in Danish.

Finnish Americans frequently organized theater groups to provide a creative outlet for their members. Irja Laaksonen, who came to the United States in 1907 when she was four, recalled her parents' participation in the Finn hall theater of Fitchburg, Massachusetts.

The Finnish Hall in Fitchburg was named "Saima Hall," after one of Finland's largest and prettiest rivers. The hall was always alive with activity. Papa spent most of his evenings there directing Finnish plays which were enjoyed by actors and audiences alike.

Mama was a wonderful actress, but she soon had to give up acting in Papa's plays because she was expecting another baby. She still took part, however, by being the "prompter." She would sit in the "prompter's box" which was hidden in the floor at the front of the stage, and if an actor forgot his lines, she would loudly whisper them to him.

Whenever a play needed children, Papa expected us to act the parts. I remember one play in particular in which all four of us were acting. We were supposed to go to sleep on a pile of straw at the front of the stage. Everything was going along fine until my little sister Ilma, who was only three years old, saw Mama sitting in the prompter's box. She squatted down in front of the box and asked, "What are you doing in there, Mama?" The audience just roared!...

Papa's fame as a play director spread to the nearby cities, and soon he was being asked to direct plays at the Finnish Hall in Quincy, Massachusetts. Eventually the Finns in Quincy offered Papa a full-time job as a play director. This was the kind of work he loved to do so we decided to move again.

One morning, just before we left Fitchburg, I woke up early and the first thing I saw was a huge basket of flowers. Where had they come from? Papa and Mama were still asleep. Dying with curiosity, I crept into their bedroom. Papa lay on his back, snoring loudly with his hands folded on his chest. On his index finger was a brand new signet ring. Later I learned that there had been a farewell party for Papa and Mama at the hall. The flowers and ring were good-bye presents from the Finns in Fitchburg. The ring was too large for Papa but he never got around to making it smaller. He always wore it on his index finger.

ELLEN PETERSON'S SWEDISH MEATBALLS

INGREDIENTS

1-2 slices rye bread

1/2 cup milk

1 egg

1/2 lb. ground beef

1/2 lb. ground pork

1/4 lb. ground veal

1 Tbs. allspice

1 Tbs. salt

1 tsp. white pepper

3 cloves garlic, minced fine

1 medium onion, minced fine or run through a food processor

1/4 cup parsley leaves, chopped very fine

3-4 Tbs. butter

3 Tbs. flour

2 cups chicken broth

Put first three ingredients in a mixing bowl and let stand until bread is soggy. Pound until mushy. Add more milk if necessary. Put all the other ingredients except the butter, flour, and broth into the bowl and mix with your hands. (It is important to use your hands because fat will stick to them and make the meatballs leaner.) When the meat is thoroughly mixed, melt 1 Tbs. butter in a skillet over medium heat. With your fingers, make meatballs about the size of large marbles (1 inch diameter) and drop into skillet. Keep shaking skillet to prevent the meatballs from sticking. When browned outside, test for doneness. Keep cooked meatballs warm in oven while preparing another batch. Add more butter with each batch. When finished, use the pan crust to make gravy by adding 3 Tbs. flour to make a paste and then gradually mixing in 2 cups broth.

Food was the element of life that most reflected the ethnic background of immigrant Americans. This Seattle delicatessen, owned by Grethe and John Petersen, sold meats and dairy products prepared in a Danish style.

Sigurd John Arthur Wiebe and his wife, Agnes Constantia Landin, with their son, John Sigurd. The couple met and married in the United States in 1902, soon after each had immigrated from Sweden.

The wedding-day portrait of Kusti Korhonen and Anna Kettunen Korhonen, both Finnish immigrants. They met in the United States, where Kusti labored in a lumber camp and Anna worked as a domestic before they bought a farm in Maine. It was customary for men to wear flowers in their lapels for weddings.

FAMILY

When immigrant men decided they were prosperous enough to marry, they often sent for sweethearts they had left at home. Sometimes, the hopeful memories lasted a long time, as the following letters, sent to the pastor of a rural church in Sweden in 1907, show.

The undersigned wishes herewith to ask whether the Pastor knows if there is any woman by the name of Anna Katarina Bergstedt. That was her maiden name about twenty-four years ago. I would like to know where she is. If the Pastor would be so kind and inform me where she is I am sending herewith a letter to her.... She lived at Vedlösa at the above-named time and her father was a miller. I am sending the Pastor an America-dollar for the trouble....

Dear Anna,

I wonder how you have it and if you are living. I have it very good here. It is a long time since we saw each other. Are you married or unmarried? If you are unmarried, you can have a good home with me. I have my own house in town and I make over ten *kronor* a day. My wife died last year in the fall and I want another wife. I only have one girl, eleven years old. If you can come to me I will send you a ticket and travel money for the spring when it will be good weather. We live very good here in America.... You must wonder who I am. My name is Einar, who worked over at Vensta for Adolf Johanson when you were at Andersons', and you were my first girl-friend. If you can't come maybe you know somebody else who wants to become a good housewife. If these lines should reach you please write right away and let me know how things are with you....

I will write a few words in English, *I am Loved joy of all my Hart j hav bin driming af bort joy y hoppes dat joy vill bi my vife....j am sand joy one worm kiss.*

The harsh conditions of pioneer life sometimes put a strain on marriages. The following two selections are from letters written by Natalie Bering, who left Denmark a year after her fiancé, Johannes Jung. The first was written on November 4, 1874, shortly after their wedding in Hastings, Nebraska. The second was written the following February.

The wedding was held in Nielsen's [a neighbor's] little sitting room with no one but the witnesses, but we were all as jolly as could be, so I did not feel I was alone without my family and without one single friend! I got myself a friend who must and will be a good one for the rest of my life. We now live in a tiny little house: 11 feet square, only one room and in that we have kitchen, bed chamber and sitting room; there I wash and bake, there we live and breathe—and although it is anything but cozy, I am well satisfied. If only we have our daily bread, everything will be all right; no matter how simple the home is, it is 10 times better than working for strangers.

I am very often alone all day and lately have begun to feel very depressed. Small wonder, when you think that I have only been married a little over three months and already have to let out all my dresses for a certain reason. Isn't that terrible? I am certain it will be exactly nine months after the wedding.... But I am not afraid. It must be nature's way that I am not afraid, in spite of the fact that I have every reason to be: 30 years old, and I am so thin and slight. Johannes is not happy either, partly because he is worried about me, that is, I guess, the main reason, and partly because it will mean some expense and a lot of trouble and suffering with a screaming baby. I am not at all sure how I shall keep the child from freezing to death.

Thorstina Walters, daughter of Icelandic immigrants, described growing up in North Dakota. Her mother was the local midwife, and Walters recalled life with a mother who worked outside of the home from time to time.

My earliest reaction to this outside work of my mother's was rebellion. Why did she not stay at home like other mothers? At times when she was on the point of answering a call I registered my disapproval so vehemently that my father and grandfather objected strenuously to taking care of me at home. Most of these calls for my mother came at night, so, if the night was cold I was summarily wrapped up snugly in one or another of the Icelandic feather ticks that were around the house, and off I went with my mother on her errand of mercy wherever it might be....

Many things went wrong on the home front during mother's frequent absences so it was fortunate that she was blessed with a sense of humor and could turn a dire domestic catastrophe into a joke. Once when the cows were not giving much milk, she had been carefully saving cream for churning and had almost filled a large crock when she was suddenly called away for two days. Upon her return she discovered that the precious cream that was

An Icelandic American family in North Dakota around 1895. Icelanders had a high degree of literacy, and they brought their long literary tradition to the United States. Although the Icelandic American community was small, it supported several Icelandic-language newspapers and at least one publishing house.

Norwegian Americans Ole and Marie Gjevre relax at home with their friend Kari Erickson. Ole strums the guitar while the women quilt. Playing an instrument was one way to while away the long hours of the prairie winter.

Christmas, or Julefest, is always a very special occasion in Scandinavian American communities. This Danish home in Racine, Wisconsin, is decorated with a Christmas tree adorned with Danish flags and traditional paper ornaments.

to be turned into golden butter had been fed to the pigs. Another time, my grandfather and I were going to surprise her by having the churning done when she came back. Inadvertently we had the old churn too full; when we went zealously to work with the dasher, the cream expanded until the lid blew off and mother's clean kitchen floor was a river of frothy, white foam. As luck would have it, she walked in just at that moment.

Looking back, I realize that mother could repair damage and restore order out of disorder in an incredibly short time. But there were times in the midst of restoring order out of chaos when she had to realize that she was tired. She would then call me, if the weather was mild, and we would go outside, wander among the trees, admire the flowers and listen to the birds. Or, if it was cold, we would go upstairs; she would set herself in her upholstered rocker by the dormer window, and set the spinning-wheel in motion. Watching her gracefully manipulate the soft wool and seeing it change into yarn was fascinating. After some time mother would feel relaxed enough to continue her interrupted household tasks.

Swedish women in Greeley County, Kansas, enjoy coffee time with cookies and bulla, or rolls—an important part of the daily routine.

Kristina Carlson Johnson immigrated from Sweden to the Dakota Territory in 1887. In 1954, her daughter Hulda recalled the delicious foods her mother had made.

Mother would make up a great deal of the best sausage imaginable, five or six varieties besides the usual head cheese. That involved a great deal of work. She was very particular about each item and she received many compliments on her sausages and meat preparations. She showed many neighbors how to prepare them. In those days there was the pork barrel for curing meat. Father also had a smokehouse where he used cobs, together with a little hickory or other wood [burning them for smoke].... Sometimes a little beef was cured and dried, which was very tasty. Mother was also known for her good bread, of which she baked many varieties, white, rye, graham, Swedish Limpa [sweet rye bread] and various rolls for certain occasions, especially at Christmastime.

Later, when milk became more plentiful, she also made cheeses for family use. It was made from sweet, whole milk, which included the cream with rennet added. The most difficult part of that was in the proper pressing and curing. Sometimes she would add anise, caraway seeds, cardamon, and cumin seed, of which Father was very fond.

Peter Kekonnen came to the United States from Finland in 1905 when he was 16 years old. Three years later, he married a young Finnish American woman, and they had four children. As an old man, Kekonnen told an interviewer how tragedy struck his family.

In February 1918 there was a terrible flu epidemic that went all over the world. Maybe you've heard of it? One evening I came in from the barn and we all had supper together as usual and went to bed. In the morning none of us could get up—Solveig, the children, and I. We were all very sick. It was a high fever, very high. We were very weak and it was hard to breathe. The neighbors heard our cows mooing and came over in the later afternoon and found us. Solveig was the worst of us all. She was out of her head with the fever. Next morning the neighbors took her on the sleigh to the depot eight miles away; and then on the train to the town where there was a hospital.

The children and I stayed in the cabin. We were sick, but not as sick as Solveig. The neighbors took care of our animals and chickens and brought us a pot of soup and some bread every afternoon. They were afraid to come in because of the sickness, but they would open the door and put the food inside and then go. One day the man came with the soup and the bread, and, after putting it down, he stood inside the door for a while, not talking. Finally he said, "I have to tell you Solveig is dead. She died in the hospital in the town...." They buried her with the other flu victims in a graveyard near the hospital. She was twenty-seven years old.

In a few weeks I was stronger and began doing the work of the farm again. I had the four children to take care of now. The oldest was nine, and Christian, who was the youngest, was only three. The neighbor woman brought bread for us still, but after a while I thought, "This isn't right. They have to take care of themselves and I have to take care of us." So one morning I made the bread myself. I had seen Solveig do it often enough, and my mother too, in the old country. I did the farmwork and chopped the wood and fed the children and cooked and washed the clothes. And in the fall I gathered the cranberries and blueberries and put them in bottles—and some of the vegetables, too. I did everything myself until Nellie was old enough to help me. And, as the boys grew, they helped, too.

Mildred "Babe" Didrikson Zaharias, the daughter of Norwegian immigrants, became an outstanding athlete. She recalled her childhood in Beaumont, Texas, in the 1920s.

I had a wonderful childhood. That must prove that it doesn't take money to be happy, because the Didriksons sure weren't rich. My father and mother had to work and scrimp and save like anything just to be able to feed and clothe us all. Poppa's trade there in Beaumont was furniture refinishing. He did fine cabinet work, and most of the time he was making

Dr. Harriet (originally Hrefna) G. McGraw was the seventh daughter of Icelandic parents who settled in Canada in the 1880s. Soon afterward, her father died, and her mother was forced to send the children to live with relatives. Hrefna traveled to Mountain, Dakota Territory, where a great-aunt lived. Years later, she cherished a letter from her grandmother in Iceland that gave her the advice that made her decide to attend medical school.

Neglect not the gifts within you, be content only with the best. Do not allow the lure of the white lights to confuse you and lead you astray and destroy the finer life and beauty of the soul. Remember that your genealogy is traceable to King Olaf the White and Queen Aud of Dublin. Be worthy of your ancestry. Be not content with husks, do not squander your time, it is precious. Improve every minute in useful, healthful work, not only for yourself, but do something worthwhile for others. Improve and achieve, my child, I trust you and I love you so much, do not disappoint us. The Almighty is with you.

Grandmother Solrun

Mrs. Andrew A. Olson makes lutefisk *at her home in St. Paul, Minnesota, in 1936. Scandinavian American families often serve the distinctive dried fish, cured in lye, at holidays.*

This Danish courting couple chats in front of the Elsinore Hotel in Salt Lake City. Many Danes converted to Mormonism and immigrated to Utah, the center of Mormon life. Today, Danish Americans make up almost 10 percent of the state's population.

The Petersens—father and three children—with their horses. They pose with pride on their farm in Danevang, a Danish American town in Texas.

around $200 a month. That was pretty good money in those days, but with seven kids to support, he generally didn't have any dimes or quarters to hand out to us for picture shows and all that.

So Poppa said, "Well, I'll build good bodies for them." He set up a regular gymnasium in the back yard. He put up bars for jumping and all that. In the garage he had this weightlifting device. It was an old broomstick with a flatiron at each end. He put it there for the boys, so they could strengthen their muscles, but my sister Lillie and I would get in there and work out with it too....

We'd play baseball in our back yard, and sometimes the ball would go into the rose bushes. Poor Momma nearly died, because she really loved her roses. I'm the same way about roses myself. Momma kept telling us to keep that baseball out of her flower beds. Then one day we persuaded her to get in the game herself. She hit a ball right into the rose bushes. We never heard any more complaints from her about our ballplaying after that....

When I got to be a sports champion, Poppa would kid around and say, "Well, she must get it from me." But I think that as far as athletics are concerned, I probably took after my mother. I understand she was considered the finest woman ice skater and skier around her part of Norway. When she was little, her dad couldn't afford to buy her skis, so he made her a pair out of barrel staves. She'd get on them and go like the wind from where she lived down into the city.

John W. Anderson, a labor organizer, was the grandson of Norwegian immigrants. Born in 1906 in an area 200 miles northwest of Milwaukee, he described the hardships that his family faced.

My most vivid childhood experience is of a terrible forest fire that swept over our farm and the surrounding area in early August 1910. There had been no rain for a period of forty days. Our nearest neighbors were a mile away. The one to the west had been clearing land. He let a brush fire get out of control.

My father, like the rest of these part-time farmers, had no knowledge of how to fight a forest fire. Hardly more than an hour before this holocaust swept across the landscape burning our house, barn and most of the livestock, my father put us on a wagon and took us down to the lake located on the southern part of the farm. A neighbor from the south of us joined my father in protecting us from the fire. We children were made to lie on a bog on the edge of the lake. We were covered with a blanket. My father and the neighbor kept throwing buckets of water on us, on each other, and on the wagon and horses standing at the edge of the lake.

My mother narrowly escaped death in the flames when she tried to save some of the cattle by driving them into the lake. We found several cows burned to death within a hundred yards of where we lay. I remember seeing the flames shooting hundreds of feet in the air over the lake. All that we saved was a team of horses with the wagon, a few belongings and a cow. For hours after the fire there were burning embers everywhere. As far as the eye could

A double wedding in the
Norwegian town of
Springfield, Iowa. Such
occasions brought out the
entire community.

see the landscape was black, not a green tree or bush in sight.

This fire was a harsh turning point in the life of our family. We went to stay with my grandparents who lived about seven miles from the farm. My grandmother had married again. After a week or so the rest of the family went back to the farm to build a log house and barn before winter set in. I lived with my grandparents for almost four years.

My grandmother was a domineering woman. Although her profane and derogatory remarks were in Norwegian, I soon learned what she meant. She sometimes pulled my ears if I didn't immediately do as I was told.

The midsummer festival was a tradition among all the Scandinavian people. Ruth Engelmann, born around 1920 to Finnish American parents, recalled her family's celebration.

Every year we celebrated the arrival of summer just as the Finns had celebrated in Finland, or so Grandmother said.... Father hitched old Maud [their horse] to a sledge and went into the woodlot to look for young maples. By afternoon, he had enough to build the midsummer leaf house. He dug potholes in the yard on the east side of the house, stuck the maples into the holes and we stamped the ground tight around the trunks. By late afternoon. the leaf house was done—three sides of maple trees and one side of our house, the benches made of sawhorses and planks, and the old wobbly kitchen table braced against the wall—all ready for us. We said it was the most beautiful leaf house we had ever had, but we always said that, every year. And every year, on the Eve of Midsummer, Hank heated the sauna, and just as night was falling we went there with our clean nightclothes wrapped in a towel....

For a whole week, sometimes until the Fourth of July, we children lived in the leaf house. Mother cooked supper outside so that our real house would stay cool for the night, but early in the morning when I was still not quite awake, I could hear the muffled sound of her pounding the cardamom seed, of slapping the cake dough with a big wooden spoon, and I knew she had heated the big stove to bake sweet biscuits and lemon cake.

The Alex Kivelas, a Finnish family in Sebeka, Minnesota, fly a U.S. flag from their car to demonstrate their patriotic feelings in the post–World War I period.

SCHOOL

The fourth-grade class of the Trimountain Grade School in Michigan is in session for the 1925–26 school year. Many of the children in this class in the state's Upper Peninsula were of Finnish descent.

Andreas A. Hjerpeland immigrated to Fillmore County, Minnesota, in 1870, when he was 35. He had attended a teacher's college in Norway and found his services in demand. For 10 years he traveled to Norwegian American communities from Minnesota to the West Coast. In 1877, he wrote to one of his former instructors in Norway, describing the life of a traveling teacher.

I came here [Lanesboro, Minnesota] late in September and began teaching October first. Since then I have taught school the whole time, that is for seven months, and have gotten twenty dollars per month plus board and washing....

According to your wishes, I will tell you a bit about the school system here. There are public schools everywhere, where the ordinary school subjects are taught: reading, writing, arithmetic, geography, and grammar. School is held in well-equipped schoolhouses, usually for seven or eight months of the year. The cities are full of higher schools and universities, so the youth have good opportunities for learning. Because there is freedom of religion, and no state church, the public schools have no religious instruction, leaving that up to the parents themselves. This is the reason the Norwegians, as well as other nationalities, establish parochial schools, so that the children will receive religious instruction. But the parochial schools have a low status.... There are not enough qualified teachers, the school session is too short, and the buildings are poor. It is quite difficult to hold Norwegian school here, and twenty dollars a month is considered poor pay here in America.

Huldah Johnson Simonette was the daughter of Swedish immigrants who settled in the Dakota Territory. She remembered what school was like for her brother Henry in 1889.

That spring Henry was six and was sent to school with only a slate and a pencil. The teacher was a Miss Susie Swift. There were about twenty-eight pupils, many of whom were grown boys. Teaching in those days was a tremendous task, requiring plenty of tact and ingenuity. The salary was from $18 to $20 a month or less. Everyone furnished his own books and supplies, which meant a variety of almost nothing....

At first Henry learned all the letters of the alphabet, numbers, and many words, as well as spelling, from an almanac which belonged to Miss Swift. She said that his progress was very good. It must have been a good beginning as he graduated from the eighth grade at the head of the class; he later taught school himself. As for the health of the school children, except for the usual colds, chill blains [skin irritation caused by the cold] and sore throats, all was well. Another early teacher was Mrs. Ed Pettys, who with her aged mother and small children and one baby, occupied the old Sedgwick house.... She would go home at noon, one mile from

The boy on top of this schoolhouse in North Dakota is raising the flag at the beginning of the school day. Prairie schools like these often drew children from many miles away, and some traveled in buggies to get there.

the school house, to care for the baby, leaving instructions with the school children to resume their studies at the proper time until she returned, many times at two o'clock. Needless to say, pandemonium reigned in the meantime.

A school term was usually six months long, three in the fall and three in the spring. Those early teachers must have done a good job, for from this early school came many teachers, an editor and publisher, an attorney, religious and educational leaders, and successful farmers, ranchers and businessmen.

Mother was very particular about school attendance. We children were never absent or tardy without a good reason. We walked one and one-half miles to school. Learning the English language was not too difficult for adults as all children in the neighborhood learned it fast and well; they spoke it more fluently than the mother tongue...and as the children talked English at home, their parents soon learned it as well.

John W. Anderson remembered his schooling in a rural area of Wisconsin in the early 20th century.

My six years in the Heineman school were not happy ones. The teacher relied on the rod to punish those who failed to learn as well as those who broke the rules. I believe I got more whippings than any two children in the school. Yet even this school was better than staying home to work on the farm. We had a mile and a half to walk each way. Temperatures of thirty degrees below zero were not uncommon. Sometimes we had four feet of snow and there were no snowplows. Our school lunch, which was sometimes frozen solid, was most often bread and syrup or peanut butter. We seldom had any meat, eggs or butter. These had to be sold to the store to buy clothing and the other necessities of life we couldn't raise on the farm.

In 1921, 15-year-old Laura Foss left Denmark to live with her aunt and uncle in Seattle. She recalled going to a Danish folk school with her cousin Greta, who had accompanied her to the United States.

We heard about this Danish folk school in Solvang [California]. Greta and I decided maybe that should be O.K. So we wrote to Pastor Kristensen who was in charge, he and his wife. It was decided that we could come

Danish American folk schools sought to inspire a love for learning and an appreciation of Danish culture. There were no exams or degrees. Along with history, composition, mathematics, and literature, the schools taught drama, singing of folk songs, and gymnastics. Here, skilled gymnast Viggo Tarnow leads a class in Hutchinson, Minnesota.

down for half price…if we could help out in the kitchen and so on. We soon found out that this was all work and no play, because we had to get up early and get all the halls and steps cleaned and washed and tables set for breakfast and all that before the rest of them arrived. Then when they went to classes and what have you, then we were left with the dishes.

After two weeks, Greta took the lead; she just decided, we're paying a hundred dollars for this? So then she said to Mrs. Kristensen, "How long is this going to go on?" "What do you mean?" "Well, I meant this, we are working all the time; we never take part in anything." "Well, you better speak to my husband about that." So we did, and he was a peach of a man, so he said, "Why don't you just forget about working; we'll hire a full time girl."… So from that time on, we had a ball.

It was lectures and it was gymnastics and it was folk dancing and reading and it was handiwork. It was wonderful. That's where I met my first husband, Harald Christiansen. He had attended school the winter before, but this year he was working as a carpenter for a contractor in town. They had some little cottages in the back of the school and some of these young men were living there and boarding at the school. So then, of course, I saw him in the evenings and on Saturdays and Sundays.

Donald G. Wirtanen, the son of Finnish immigrants, was born and grew up in Markham, Minnesota. He remembered his school days during World War I.

One day soon after I started school, my teacher, who herself was of Finnish heritage, "caught" me talking Finnish during recess. She grasped me by my chin and scolded me, "I don't want to ever again hear you speaking that language." This was the result of the war hysteria of World War I. Finland was perceived to be an ally of Germany, and, therefore, Finnish, along with German, were "subversive languages." Of course I continued to speak Finnish. It was the language I spoke with my parents as long as they lived. The chin twisting didn't bother me. But I was disappointed that I didn't get the "I speak English" button which my fellow classmates

A teacher assembles her students in front of a schoolhouse in Fosston, Minnesota, in 1895 for a class picture. All the children were of Scandinavian origin, mainly Norwegian.

displayed proudly. I told this story a few years ago at the closing ceremony of a Finnish language seminar that I helped organize at our university. As a result, friends sent me "I speak English" buttons to soothe my hurt feelings of some sixty-five years earlier!

Ruth Engelmann grew up in a small Finnish American community in Wisconsin in the 1920s. As a child she suffered from eczema, a painful and itchy rash; she had to wear bandages on her hands. As she recalled, these saved her from punishment at school.

One day when the sun was bright and the dry heat shimmered above the register, my arms under the layers of bandages began to itch. I squirmed and rubbed my arms. One of the oldest girls at Revier [School], Elvi Koivunen, began to mimic every move I made. She whispered to her friends, all of them old enough to be out of our school and on to more productive tasks. Now they all began to squirm. Because I was near the washstand, I threw the water-filled basin at them, and hurled the scrub brush, the metal basket and the package of towels as well. The splashing cold water and the flying towels were as soothing as autumn leaves falling into the Montfer [River].

"Look what she did!" screamed Elvi to Miss Malone, sitting at her desk.

"I saw her," said Miss Malone. "Into the cloakroom, Mary." She followed me and closed the door tight. I sat on the cold floor and became a prisoner, a lost czarina, a sea-tossed sailor. When I could no longer stand the boredom of being alone, I climbed the stepladder to reach the top shelf of the bookcase and there I found a book, its cover faded and its pages yellowed. I brought it down and began to read the names in the table of contents. Letter by letter. Longfellow. Wordsworth. Tennyson. I knew the names! Mother had read me poems which they had written. Now, as I studied the print, familiar words and then whole sentences formed in my head.

Again and again I went into the cloakroom to pay for my misdeeds and to enjoy my imprisonment. Finally I won daily punishment. The narrow coat-filled place with its one shelf of discarded literature, history and geography books became my private schoolroom. One day Miss Malone found me asleep. I had an old geography book in my lap. "What are you doing?" she asked.

"Reading."

"Out!" said Miss Malone, as if reading were the ultimate crime a child could commit in the cloakroom of her school....

Now Miss Malone had to find a more suitable punishment for me, her "worst pupil." Her punishment could not have been better directed at my ailment. She would ask me to hold out my bandaged hand, palm up, and then she would bring down the ruler. After the first time, I drew back my hand just at the last moment, and the ruler broke as it hit the edge of my desk. She lost many rulers, for she could not bring herself to grasp my bandaged hand so that I couldn't withdraw it. I was untouchable except with a ruler.

Aagot Raaen grew up in the 1870s in a Norwegian American community in the Dakotas. On her first day of school, only one of the children understood English, which was the language the teacher spoke. At recess, the English-speaking student explained the rules the teacher had listed on the chalkboard.

1. Anyone who whispers will stay after school.

2. Anyone who laughs out loud will stay in at recess.

3. If you have to talk to anyone, raise your hand and say, "May I speak?" If you are thirsty, say, "Please may I get a drink?" If you have to go out, say, "Please may I leave the room?" The ones who never ask these questions will get better marks than those who do.

4. Anyone who speaks Norwegian in the schoolhouse or anywhere near it will be punished.

Ministers who served rural Scandinavian American communities often had many congregations and preached at different places on a regular rotation. This minister's chest held his Bible and other religious objects.

RELIGION

Mormon missionaries were quite successful in the Scandinavian countries, particularly Denmark. Many converts chose to come to the Promised Land in Utah. Mourits Petersen, a farmer from North Jutland, Denmark, wrote home to his son in 1864 from Mount Pleasant in central Utah. He indicated the strength of his new faith and a desire to convert the rest of the family.

Dear Frederik! Work as best you can so that your brothers may join in the Covenant; your endeavors to save your immortal souls give me great joy, as the day will surely come when God will reward each in accordance with his deeds.... I long to see you all here in the Lord's Promised Land; make every effort to come, as you would find joy in this wonderful land where we can serve God in peace and not be mocked. Yes, I would once again remind you to come here, and if you refuse to listen to my dear voice, you will surely regret it. My advice to you is to bend your knees and pray to God in your heart of hearts so that He will hear you and lead you here. This is a fertile land; yes, you would be filled with wonder if you could be here and see how well the people live; yes, I can say as Peter said on the mountain, this is a good place to be for those who would serve the Lord.

I must now tell you of a great sorrow that has befallen me; the Lord has taken my beloved wife. This was hard for me, but I know that if I keep the faith, she will be mine again on Judgement Day. Yes, Dear Children, I can assure you that she had an

A church picnic in a Norwegian American community in Wisconsin in the late 19th century brings together all members of the congregation. Churches formed a focal point for socializing within the immigrant communities.

easy, peaceful death. She spoke often of you before she was taken ill; she wanted to tell you of our successful journey. She had traveled over half way down the valley before she became ill; she was sick for three weeks. You must write to me as soon as you receive this letter, and let me hear of your intentions and how all of you are. I ask you, Dear Frederik, to do me the service of reading this for your brothers.

Confirmation is an important occasion in the lives of Lutherans, indicating that the person has become a full-fledged member of the religious community. Laurence Larson, who came to the United States from Norway with his family in 1870, remembered the religious training leading to his confirmation.

A group of young people, of whom I was one, assembled at the home of an old parishioner who lived not far from the county seat. I was fifteen years of age at the time and was probably one of the oldest in the class. For two or three days we sat with the pastor reading, reciting, and receiving instruction in the Lutheran way of salvation. The Reverend Mr. Thormodsgaard was kind and sympathetic, but he could brook no error on this important subject. When the question came, what does it mean to be saved? no one seemed about to reply; the good man was quite shocked. I suddenly remembered the statement in Pontoppidan's *Explanation* [a classic describing Lutheran beliefs] and the day was saved....

The following Sunday was confirmation day. It began with a dull, gray, drizzly morning and the weather did not improve as the hours went by. The long drive of ten miles in the lumber wagon was anything but delightful. At half after ten we assembled at the courthouse....

It was customary in Norway for the pastor to arrange the candidates in the order of their ability or the thoroughness of their preparation. To be first on the church floor was regarded as a signal honor. But on this occasion no attempt was made to give us definite places. We all avoided the place at the head of the line, or tried to do so. And so it fell out that this place was left for a young unfortunate fellow with a slow and dull mind, one who had been refused confirmation by another pastor because he seemed to have no adequate understanding of what the ceremony really meant.

The oral examination was brief and after the usual preliminaries the pastor proceeded to the ancient ceremonial. He began, as custom was, with the candidate at the head of the line.

"Dost thou forsake the devil?" And the youth replied with an emphatic "No."

A shock passed through the congregation. All eyes were turned on the unfortunate boy. This was something new in the lives of the worshipers. Loud sighs were heard, and with the sighs came tears.

The young man clearly wished to have nothing to do with the devil; but "forsake" was a word that had no place in his vocabulary. The pastor was nonplussed. He repeated the question

The confirmation class of the Swedish-Finnish Lutheran Church of Worcester, Massachusetts, in 1904. The pastor, John Gullans, poses with (from left) Maria Alina Carlson, Anna Olivia Carlson, and Maria Gustafson.

with the same result. He then rephrased it and stated it in terms that would require a negative answer. The boy, who had now come to understand that his first reply was wrong promptly answered, "Yes."

My turn came next and everything went well. We all declared that we had forsaken the devil and all his works and all his ways. Next we affirmed our belief in the Apostles' Creed. Then we gave the pastor our hand in token of our honest confession. A brief prayer followed. The pastor next proceeded with the celebration of the Lord's Supper, of which we now partook for the first time. I believe my unfortunate friend was privately confirmed after the close of the service.

A young Swedish American recalled his experiences as a visiting preacher in the late 19th century. He had stayed overnight at the home of "Brother F."

I looked out the window; up against the side of the house a large grocery box was set up. Round about were arranged wagon seats and planks, where a large group of people had gathered. I was told that some had come thirty-five miles. It was hot out under the blazing sun, for there was no shade. We sang and prayed and then Brother F. said, "Now the Covenant's youngest preacher will preach."

I then had to stand up on the box. Before me was a group of weather-beaten and deeply furrowed faces with that faraway gaze which is only seen among folk from the prairie. When I had preached for some forty minutes, I jumped down from the box, but then a thickset man said, "You ought to know, Pastor, that we have come a long way and that we don't have meetings so often, so please go and get up on the box again." There was nothing else to do. An equally long sermon again. Baskets and boxes were now opened. There was plenty of food. F. said, "We will go on with the meeting as soon as we have eaten." So, up on the box again. The Lord was with us. Oh, what an advantage to be able to preach for these people! When I had finished preaching, a small man stood up, who said in a hoarse voice, "Those were good, deep draughts," and then he prayed fervently to God. F. whispered to me, "That is Pastor G. Norseen." I became apprehensive, for it was said of him that he did not like young preachers. I warmly implored him to preach, but he said he would not. "No," he said, "you must get up on the box. There will not be more than four sermons in any case." There was nothing else to do.

The local church was both a community center and a religious organization. Christian Beckof of the St. Ansgar Danish Evangelical Lutheran Church in Salinas, California, noted its meaning for him.

In 1910 somebody [Mrs. Bodil Jaeger] brought a beautiful painting from Denmark and that...tells the story of the good shepherd who left the ninety and nine and went looking for the one that was lost. He found that one and brought it to the still waters.... That picture also means a lot to us. Do you know how many memories that picture brings back to all of us

The congregation appears in front of the Norway Lutheran Church, built in 1907, in rural McHenry County, North Dakota,. The architecture of this church resembles that of churches in Norway.

Sunday worship services are in progress inside this Norwegian American Lutheran Church. The official state church in all the Scandinavian countries was Lutheran. In accordance with the Norwegian custom of earlier times, the men sit on one side, the women on the other.

who are old-timers? I've seen from time to time that some of the old-timers will stand there and look at that picture and I know that if I talked to them they wouldn't have answered because they were so far back in their thought. I'll bet they had many wonderful memories.... When I look at that picture...I remember that I saw my parents kneel down in communion in front of that picture. My wife and I stood in front of that picture when we were married fifty years ago. We brought our children up there at baptism and confirmation, and I walked my daughter up the aisle in front of that picture to give her away in marriage, and I've seen my grandchildren being baptized in front of that picture. How wonderful it is to have many memories and that's only four generations. I know some of the members that talk about five or six generations' memories of this church.

Roberta Christine Kulma, the granddaughter of Finnish immigrants, grew up in Fairport Harbor, Ohio, in the 1940s. Though Fairport Harbor was dubbed "Finn Town," Irish and Italian families also lived there. She recalled the importance of the Suomi (or Finnish) Lutheran church and occasional conflicts with the local Catholics.

The Church, which played a vital role within the entire community, was another binding force. Both the Lutherans and Catholics preached to their young the evils and pitfalls of the other. We were told marriage to a Catholic would require all children to be signed over to the Pope and Catholic Church. In turn the St. Anthony nuns warned against dating "those Finn kids," and probably threatened possible excommunication and untold years in purgatory....

The "Suomi" Church (the name was later changed, much to my disappointment) was the center of both social and religious life. The children's choirs sang in English and Finnish, family dinners were sponsored by the women's group, the teenagers took part in Luther League and went to Camp Luther in the summer, and the boys played on church teams.

Raising the maypole is a tradition in all Scandinavian communities. However, because winter often lasts through May in the northern parts of some Scandinavian countries, the maypole celebration is often held at Midsummernight in June.

CHAPTER SIX

PART OF THE UNITED STATES

candinavian Americans
have made many distin-
guished contributions to
American life and culture.
Carl Sandburg, the son of
a Swedish immigrant, be-
came one of the most
popular American poets
of the 20th century.

Ole E. Rölvaag, who arrived from
Norway in 1896, wrote two novels
that were published in 1925 as *Giants
in the Earth*. Many critics think his
work is the best fictional account of
the Scandinavian immigrant experience. Rölvaag wrote in Norwegian
and had his works translated into English. He and another Norwegian
American novelist, Waldemar Ager,
cooperated in an effort to promote
the Norwegian language and culture
in the United States.

Danish immigrant Jacob Riis,
who arrived in the United States in
1870, found work as a reporter for
New York City newspapers. He
used a camera to document the hor-
rifying conditions in the city's slum
areas. Riis collected his findings in a
book, *How the Other Half Lives*
(1890), that helped gain public support for social reforms.

Thorstein Veblen, the son of
Norwegian immigrants, became a
noted economist. His book *The
Theory of the Leisure Class* (1899)
attacked what he felt was the domi-
nance of American society by big

business. Veblen's ideas formed the
basis for Franklin Roosevelt's New
Deal social programs of the 1930s.

Many Scandinavian Americans
have found success in the business
world. Vincent Bendix and George
Norman Borg (of the Borg-Warner
Company) founded important industrial manufacturing concerns. Carl
Eric Wickman started a small bus
company in Hibbing, Minnesota,
that grew into the Greyhound Bus
Lines. Philip G. Johnson, an airplane
pioneer, was president of both Boeing
and United Airlines. Johnson developed two of the most important
military airplanes of World War II,
the B-17 and B-29.

Eero Saarinen, who emigrated
from Finland in 1923 at the age of
13, formed an architectural firm with
his father, Eliel. The Saarinens were in
the forefront of modern American architecture and furniture design.
Among the many structures Eero
Saarinen designed are the Gateway
Arch in St. Louis and the headquarters of the Columbia Broadcasting
System in New York City.

Many inventions by Scandinavian
Americans have influenced daily life
in the United States. Justus P.
Seeburg invented both the jukebox
and the parking meter. Chester
Carlson, working in his New York
City apartment, developed a photocopying process that made Xerox a
name known around the world.

Charles Lindbergh gained a perma-
nent place in history on May 21,
1927, when he became the first person
to fly across the Atlantic Ocean alone.
Lindbergh was awarded the Congres-
sional Medal of Honor—usually reserved for battlefield heroism.

The son of a Swedish-born congressman from Minnesota, Lindbergh tried in vain to escape the
fame that engulfed him. In 1932, his
infant son was kidnapped and killed.
Lindbergh then went to Europe,
where he accepted an invitation to
inspect the air force of Nazi Germany. After returning home,
Lindbergh actively opposed U.S. involvement in World War II. None-
theless, he served as a technical
adviser for U.S. aircraft manufactur-
ers and flew military missions in the
Pacific during the war.

Another Scandinavian American trailblazer was Vilhjalmur
Stefansson, of Icelandic ancestry.
In the early 20th century, Stefansson made a series of trips to the
Arctic. There, he lived among the
native people, the Inuit, studying
their customs. On Victoria Island, he encountered a group
with blond hair and blue eyes. He
believed that they were descendants of the Scandinavian
colonists of Greenland.

The sports world has also had its
share of Scandinavian American heroes. Knute Rockne, born in Nor-

way in 1888, came to the United States with his parents five years later. As a player and later coach of the football team at the University of Notre Dame, Rockne made the team into a national football power and compiled a winning record few other coaches have ever approached.

Babe Didrikson Zaharias is regarded by many as the greatest American woman athlete. Barely out of high school, she won two gold medals (in the javelin throw and 80-meter hurdles) at the 1932 Olympic Games in Los Angeles. That same year, she won six track and field events at the national U.S. amateur competition. She later became a golfer, winning 17 consecutive tournaments in 1946–47. Her brilliant career was cut short by cancer in 1956, when Zaharias was only 42.

Many Scandinavian Americans have become artists, but perhaps none created a more enduring work than Gutzon Borglum. Born in Idaho of Danish immigrant parents in 1871, Borglum spent 14 years creating the four huge heads of George Washington, Abraham Lincoln, Thomas Jefferson, and Theodore Roosevelt on Mount Rushmore in South Dakota. Borglum died in 1941, leaving the work only partially finished. His son Lincoln completed it.

Claes Oldenburg, born in Sweden in 1929, arrived in the United States seven years later. Starting an artistic career in the 1950s, he had a great influence on modern art and is best known for his giant sculptures of such everyday objects as hamburg-

ers, light switches, and lipsticks.

Scandinavian Americans have also gained fame as popular entertainers. Swedish-born movie star Greta Garbo retired in 1939, but her beauty created a legend that lasted till her death in 1990. Victor Borge, a Danish immigrant, delighted audiences from the 1940s to the 1980s with his blend of piano music and comedy. Ozzie and Harriet Nelson, with their sons David and Ricky, starred in one of the first television family comedies in the 1950s. Ricky grew up to become a rock star, and today three of his children are also in show business.

Children in Swedish clothing fill the main square of Lindsborg, Kansas, during Hyllingsfest, *a celebration honoring ancestors.*

Edgar Bergen, a ventriloquist, appeared on both radio and television with his two "dummies," Mortimer Snerd and Charlie McCarthy. His daughter Candice Bergen progressed from child star to an Emmy Award–winning TV sitcom actress. Ann-Margret Olssen, born in Sweden in 1941, discarded her last name when she became a singer and movie star in the United States.

Scandinavian Americans form a relatively small part of the nation's population, but because they are con-

centrated in a few states, they have been able to exercise political power. The most successful Scandinavian American politician of the 19th century was Knute Nelson. Born in Norway, he arrived in the United States with his mother in 1849 when he was six. He served in the Wisconsin state legislature in 1868 and then moved to Minnesota. There he became the first Scandinavian American elected to the U.S. House of Representatives (1882), the first Scandinavian governor of the state (1892), and finally the first Scandinavian U.S. senator from Minnesota (1895), a post that Nelson held for 28 years.

One key to Nelson's political success was his ability to attract votes from all Scandinavian American groups. Swedish Americans found that the tactic worked for them, too. Swedish-born John Lind was elected to the U.S. House of Representatives from Minnesota in 1886. Twelve years later, he became the state's first Swedish governor.

More recently, several Scandinavian Americans have made their mark on national politics. Earl Warren, born in Los Angeles of a Norwegian father and a Swedish mother, served as California's governor from 1943 to 1953. He was the Vice Presidential candidate on the losing Republican ticket in 1948. In 1953, President Dwight D. Eisenhower named Warren chief justice of the United States, a position he held until his death in 1969.

President Franklin D. Roosevelt claimed that he had two Swedish ancestors, but no other Scandinavian American has reached the nation's highest office. Two politicians of Scandinavian heritage, Hubert Humphrey and Walter Mondale, served as Vice Presidents in Democratic administrations. But both men failed in their own campaigns for the Presidency (Humphrey in 1968, Mondale in 1984). John B. Anderson, an Illinois Congressman whose father came from Sweden, ran as an independent candidate for President in 1980. He received 5.7 million votes, 7 percent of those cast.

In 1938, to commemorate the 300th anniversary of the founding of the Swedish colony in Delaware, Swedish Americans organized celebrations in many communities. Sweden's crown prince (later King Gustav VI Adolf) visited the Minnesota State Fairgrounds, where more than 100,000 people had gathered.

That same year, Kate Bearnson Carter, the daughter of Icelandic immigrants, sponsored the construction of a lighthouse in Spanish Fork, Utah. It was a monument to the first Icelandic American settlers.

Scandinavian Americans have continued to honor their heritage with celebrations throughout the nation. May 17, Norwegian Independence Day, is marked by parades and feasts in Brooklyn, Chicago, Minneapolis, Seattle, and many other places. Norwegian Americans also celebrate October 9, the date that the first group of Norwegian immigrants arrived in New York City in 1825.

On the Saturday closest to Columbus Day, Chicago's Swedish Americans celebrate Leif Eriksson Day, in honor of the explorer who arrived in America 500 years before Columbus. A young man or woman marches down Clark Street ringing a bell. The procession continues with folk singers and dancers in their ancestors' native costumes. Shopkeepers bring out corn-brooms painted blue and yellow, the colors of the Swedish flag.

June 5, Danish Constitution Day, is celebrated in Chicago; Minneapolis; Croton, New York; and San

Norwegian-born Kirsten Tollefson of Bay Ridge, Brooklyn (shown here with her husband), is a folk artist who made the doll and embroidered the pillows on the couch using traditional Norwegian patterns.

Rafael, California. Solvang, California, a town in which the buildings resemble those in Denmark, has a gala "Danish Days" celebration in September.

The anniversary of Icelandic Independence Day, June 17, 1944, is celebrated by many Icelandic Americans. Spanish Fork, Utah, where the early Icelandic Mormons settled, is still a center of the Icelandic American community.

Each year, Finnish Americans gather in a different place for FinnFest, a four-day event that celebrates the Finnish culture and language. Such groups as the Kalevala Players of Berkeley (California) perform plays, and Finnish American children sing traditional Finnish songs. Finnish dishes are served, and people from far-flung Finnish American communities renew old ties.

Finnish Americans celebrate March 16 as St. Urho's Day. The legend of St. Urho parallels that of St. Patrick, whose feast (not by coincidence) falls on the following day. Supposedly, St. Urho waved his pitchfork and drove the grasshoppers out of Finland, much as St. Patrick drove the snakes from Ireland. Finnish Americans cheerfully admit that the story of St. Urho is of recent origin. He appeared in a "vision" to Professor Sulo Havumaki of Bemidji State University in Minnesota. Finnish Americans have "discovered" buried relics of the saint, indicating that he, too, immigrated to America.

Finally, Scandinavian Americans insist that the idea of honoring Christopher Columbus as the "discoverer" of America is erroneous. Since 1928, North Dakota has celebrated October 12 as Discoverers' Day in honor of Columbus and Leif Eriksson.

A new generation of Norwegian Americans displays the Norwegian flag at the Norway Day parade in Bay Ridge, Brooklyn, in 1995. Norway Day, May 17, celebrates Norway's independence from Sweden and is also a time when Norwegian Americans gather to celebrate their heritage.

TIES WITH THE HOMELAND

Amandus Johnson was born in Småland, Sweden, in 1877. Two years later, his family emigrated to the United States, settling in Minnesota. In 1906, Johnson returned to Sweden to gather information about the 17th-century Swedish American colony for his doctoral dissertation at the University of Pennsylvania.

When I first arrived I had actually been disappointed. The thing was that my grandfather in Minnesota had always described Sweden to me as a paradise. His heart was back in Sweden and as the years passed he increasingly idealized conditions back home, which in all ways seemed to him much better than in America, even when it was a question of such things as fruit and fish. Apples in America tasted like nothing compared with the juicy apples in Småland, strawberries in Sweden tasted much better than our American ones, and the pike in Långasjö were so marvelous that it was a shame to compare them with the fish in Minnesota. I listened to Grandfather's descriptions and as a child thought about them a great deal, and in my mind told myself, "Some day...some day...I will travel to Sweden...I will taste the apples and strawberries in paradise and the good fish that can be caught in Långasjö and which is better than any other fish."...

I had expected that everything in Sweden would be large and magnificent, in accordance with Grandfather's descriptions. This turned out not to be so. The little red cottages along the road were picturesque but not imposing. The trees were small in comparison with the giant trees I had seen in various places in America, the locomotives were much smaller than our American

"Greetings from Hallingdal" (a town in Norway) adorns Orville Bakken's car in a Fourth of July parade in North Dakota.

engines, the same with the streetcars. But everything was clean and proper and there were flower beds around the railroad stations. A little railroad station in America in those days looked like a junk heap in comparison with a Swedish one—here trash lay in piles and there were no flowers. The villages in Sweden were not so different from small communities in America, but everything was cleaner and neater, and there were flowers everywhere.

Earl Warren, who became chief justice of the United States, was born in Los Angeles in 1891. His mother was from Sweden and his father from Norway. In 1953, Warren made a trip to Scandinavia with his wife and daughters, as he recalled in his memoirs.

My mother had been born in the province of Hälsingland, not far from Sundsvall. The farm and the home in which she was born were still in the family. Through the vicar of the church in the area, we were invited to a family gathering at the home. There must have been nearly a hundred relatives there of all ages. We did not know any of them because my mother had sailed from there as a babe in arms in 1866, and had had no connection with any of them since coming to the United States. We were taken to the fjord from which my grandparents had sailed, and were told that until a year or two before our arrival there was an old man who remembered, and often told about, seeing the ship that carried them, their family, and other Swedish emigrants to America. The younger members of the family group were dressed in their colorful festive garments, and we were entertained with the folk dances and songs of the region. We were told much family history that we had never heard before, and, as a departing gift, the vicar, on behalf of our relatives, presented us with a nice leather folder containing a record of the title to the farm, showing it had been in the family at least since 1607....

We traveled by car...to Norway, where we saw many of the beautiful fjords between Trondheim and Stavanger. We stopped at Haugesund, where my father was born. The mayor of the city arranged for a reception in the City Hall of all my father's relatives whom he could muster. Again, we knew none of them because my father also was a babe in arms when he sailed to America about ninety years before. We were happy to see these good people and enjoyed the gathering. Then we visited the little farm from which my grandparents emigrated to America. I could understand why they left. The farm was not only small, but even in summer, when things should look their best, the place did not appear to be very productive; certainly not as much as the cornfields of Iowa where they eventually went to live.

This 4-ton statue of a Viking is 28 feet high and stands in Alexandria, Minnesota. "Big Ole" proclaims the town as the country's oldest, a declaration based on the belief that the Vikings had traveled this far inland.

Peter Martins

"To me, dancing is a total expression of myself," Peter Martins once said in an interview. The ballet dancer was born in Copenhagen, Denmark, in 1946. His father was an engineer and his mother a pianist. When Peter was seven, he accompanied his two sisters to an audition for the Royal Danish Ballet School. The school did not need any more girls, but it unexpectedly accepted Peter.

Peter hated the school's discipline and often rebelled against its strict training. He had little time for play. Still, he became an *aspirant,* the term for an apprentice or beginning dancer. He worked to improve his strength and endurance by taking up tennis and soccer and working out with weights. When he was 18, he was accepted as the youngest principal dancer in the Royal Danish Ballet. Even in his early performances, he was known for his excellent technique and form.

In 1967, Martins attracted the attention of George Balanchine, director of the New York City Ballet. One of the dancers in Balanchine's troupe became ill before a performance in Edinburgh, Scotland, and Martins took on the role. Balanchine was impressed and invited Martins to appear as a guest artist with the New York City Ballet.

At first, things were not easy for Martins. Balanchine had his own style of dancing that was quite different from the Danish style. In addition, Balanchine's personality was abrasive, and Martins suffered from his frequent criticism. By the mid-1970s, however, Martins was one of the company's primary dancers. He was often paired with Suzanne Farrell, the leading female dancer. In 1977, *Dance* magazine cited Martins as "the personification of the premier *danseur noble.*" His good looks made him a media star as well.

Martins hoped someday to become director of a major ballet company. But when the Royal Danish Ballet offered him the job in 1976, he turned it down. He did not believe he was ready.

Around that time, Martins began his first efforts with choreography, creating his own ballets. After Balanchine's death in 1983, Martins accepted the post of codirector of the New York City Ballet. Ten years later he became sole director. Many dance critics believe he will one day surpass the achievements of his mentor.

Frederik Madsen emigrated from Denmark in 1922 at the age of 17. Fifty years later, he returned with his wife, who was also Danish American.

That was a wonderful trip. We were in Denmark three, four weeks and everyday was a banquet. You can't go to Denmark without gaining weight; it's just impossible. They sure know how to put on a festivity. Every place we went, they would have a big dinner in their homes and have friends and other relatives along too. We went to a wedding and I got up to make a little speech in Danish. But I spoke dialect. And they had not heard that dialect for many years!

Many Scandinavian Americans retain their ties to family members in the old countries. Henny Hale, who emigrated by herself in 1923 and settled in Tacoma, Washington, described her efforts to keep in touch.

I have been back to Norway twice. In 1977 I went for the first time and in 1979 I took my two daughters with me for the family reunion; that was a joyous trip. They say when you have been away from home, anything looks different and smaller. Well, that is not just imagination. I am so sure that all the hills were smaller, absolutely. The hills where I used to run chasing the cows and the sheep, they were smaller and they were much rockier and the river where I used to go swimming was a trickle. But I took my girl up to that place where I stood on tiptoe [the moment when she decided to come to the United States] and that was quite some moment.

In 1939, the Soviet Union invaded Finland, expecting to defeat the much smaller nation easily. The Finns resisted heroically in what became known as the Winter War. Finnish Americans sent aid to the beleaguered nation. Paula Ivaska Robbins, who grew up in Bergen County, New Jersey, recalled those days.

For a number of years during the early years of the War, we sent packages of food to our relatives in Finland, especially my grandparents, who had burned their farm in Karjala to the ground rather than permit it to be taken over by the invading Russians. Preparing the packages became an important ritual in our little family. During the week before a package left, mother picked up a sturdy cardboard carton from the grocery store and purchased non-perishable items that would travel well, mostly canned goods. Always, of course, there were several tins of coffee. After dinner Mother and Father would spread all of the groceries out on the dining table, and then pack everything into the box as tightly as they could, filling in the spaces with soft things such as pairs of wool socks or handkerchiefs. Then the box would be taped shut. It was then wrapped up in a piece of unbleached muslin, which my mother would sew closed. Finally, Father tied the whole bundle up tightly with strong twine tied in several sailor's knots, and Mother printed the address and our return address in her neat hand.

Most of the packages apparently survived their long and perilous journey across the submarine-infested waters and arrived safely, for we received many grateful letters of thanks from members of the family and lovely presents after the War. Whenever a bundle arrived, family members said they gathered together for a cup of real coffee—a special treat, since all that was available in Finland was chicory. My parents both laughed and cried over one letter in which my stepgrandfather puzzled over what kind of odd tasting American food was in that tube marked "Gillette shaving cream."

Velma Hakkila Doby, a second-generation Finnish American, is the director of the Minnesota Finnish American Family History Project. She recalled her girlhood in northern Wisconsin in the 1920s and 1930s.

Whenever neighbors, relatives, or *omanpaikaisia* (kinfolk) were visiting, after being sent to bed, I would instead stop on the stair landing, sit—elbows on my knees, chin cupped in my hands—and continue to listen to the adults reminisce about *vanhaamaata* (Old Country).... Especially impressed with Mother's poignant stories about her mother, I wondered how she had been able to leave her mother in Finland. Constantly I dreamed about some day reuniting them! When I was older, I began corresponding with Grandmother and continued until her death (four years before my first visit to Finland). A letter from Finland described Grandmother in a crude coffin, her white-gloved hands clasping a pressed rose I had included in my last letter to her. (They wondered how I had known to send a rose "just in time.")...

Beginning in 1958, I have visited Finland every four years or so and have met many [relatives]. Although I did not realize my dream of reuniting my grandmother and my mother, Mother has had the opportunity to meet a niece and nephew and some of the children. Twenty cousins have now crossed what one of them described as, "that invisible bridge Velma has constructed over the Atlantic." And more will be crossing it, both ways!

Lars Pedersen left Hellested, Denmark, in 1886 when he was 17. Sixty years later he wrote a letter to his half brother in Hellested.

Dear Brother Peder and Sister-in-law and Children. We have received your dear letter and the photograph of our old home with great pleasure. You could not have sent us a better gift for our golden wedding anniversary. Many times in my life I have thought of our old home and wished to see it again, and now I can see it almost as it was when I left my home more than 60 years ago. We have bought a good frame and have hung it up in our living room, and I am proud of it. I tell my children and friends who come here that my father built that home himself and brought up a big family there.

Gymnasts from Finland perform in a park in Worcester, Massachusetts, for a primarily Finnish-American crowd.

PRESERVING THE HERITAGE

This girl helps with the cooking in Solvang, California, also known as "Denmark in the USA." The community was founded in 1911 by a band of Danes hoping to preserve the culture of their homeland in a colony nestled in the Santa Inez Mountains.

In the early 1980s, when he was in his 70s, Frederik Madsen looked back on the importance of his Danish heritage.

In Tyler, Minnesota, they don't have folk school anymore, but they have the building and they have doings there. Every fall, they have a Danish folk meeting there that is pretty much like a week at a folk school—singing and listen to lectures and folk dancing and learn to live the good life. We learn to realize what is worthwhile in life and what isn't, to make life rich. It's only for four days and it's a long ways to go for that, but I wouldn't miss it for anything. It's really important to me because I'm together with people that think pretty much as I do. They're all people of Danish descent. Once in a while, there is somebody that has married a Dane that's gotten so Danish they come. We don't speak it so much, but some of the lectures are in Danish. Most of the singing is in Danish.

The singing part of my Danish heritage means an awful lot to me. We have a book, songbook for the Danish folk in America. It has translations from Danish. A favorite song is #290, one of Grundtvig's songs. [Nikolai Grundtvig compiled a collection of Danish ballads in the 1850s.] It's basically on playing an active life in this world. You sing about every part of life in this songbook; that's real important to me.

Gudrun Lindal Magnusson was born in the United States to Icelandic immigrant parents. In 1921, she married Jon Magnusson, who had arrived from Iceland as an infant. In the 1980s, she described some of the traditional food she taught her children and grandchildren to make.

We make *skyr*. It's served as a pudding and it's made from buttermilk. That's warmed and then strained and strained until it's the consistency that we want for pudding. Little bit of cream and little bit of sugar, and then you serve it in a little bowl with cream and sugar as the party wants. That's very popular. Of course, we're fond of fish, and that's cooked any way that the Americans do. They mostly boil it. And then the hard fish. That wasn't really considered as food, but a delicacy. Hard fish is cod, dried cod, dried so you have to beat it to be able to chew it. It has a strong taste. And *hangikjöt*, that's smoked mutton.... You serve it cold and slice it and it's very tasty.

The brown bread is a special bread. Whole wheat or partly, whatever you want, but there has to be brown wheat in it. And molasses; that's what makes it taste. You can steam it and that tastes very good or you can bake it. I used to make them both [steamed and baked], lots of brown bread. *Pönnukökur* is another delicacy. They make real thin pancakes and you roll them with sugar. Sugar is all we ever put in, but some of the Icelanders put jelly, too, or jam and berries. We had to make them thin. I have a special skillet for that.

Vinarterta, of course, was the chief coffeecake. That was sort of a cookie dough and it was baked in cake tins so it came out as layers. Then you put it with prune jam. You cooked the prunes real well, then stoned them and then put whatever flavor you wanted—lemon was one essential—and you boiled it again until it was thick. Then you see, the cakes, whether they are square or round, they're placed one on top of the other and the jam put in between. This is left to soften; it's hard to cut at first. But if you've kept it for a day or so, it cuts up better. We'd have at least five layers, [often] seven or eight. It looks nice. We cut it in layers and serve, with whipped cream is our favorite. The girls now don't do as much baking. They're keeping the recipes in case they do.

Thorstina Walters wrote about her family's love of their Icelandic heritage.

Very early in my development I became aware that there was another land that was not America, but Iceland. There it was, far off and mysterious, its language, Icelandic, generally used in my childhood home. Father had good command of written and spoken English and mother could make herself understood to a limited degree. Pretty soon I was being told many things in connection with the two countries. Grandfather, *"afi,"* related how he braved the turbulent ocean in small rowboats loading them with precious fish. He managed to describe the ocean and its moods in such a telling way that the child of the prairies acquired a picture of it. Now and then he sketched the mountains, sometimes gleaming in colors that were vibrant and gay in the rarefied northern air, at other times dark and brooding, giving rise to tales of trolls and hidden-folks, ghosts and other mystic beings, belonging only to Iceland, certainly not at home on the plain of North Dakota. Grandfather enjoyed telling me about the fire that was always at work beneath the Icelandic soil. He described the Great Geyser, the famous hot spring of Iceland, which sends up a column of hot water rising to a height of 150 to 200 feet, each eruption lasting as long as twenty minutes. Grandfather went to a great deal of trouble explaining this phenomenon to me, not forgetting to tell me that all great hot springs in the world were named after the Icelandic *"Geysir,"* the grandest of them all....

Among Grandfather's stories were those of mid-summer excursions into the interior to gather the famous *"fjallagrös"* (Iceland moss). These outings were particularly enjoyed by the young people, tenting out on the heaths, whiling away the bright summer evenings in songs, games and dances. Of course they did not forget to bring home quantities of the far-famed

Norman Borlaug

Norman Borlaug, a Norwegian American, was the first agricultural scientist to win the Nobel Peace Prize. He was honored in 1970 for his contributions to the green revolution. Borlaug's discoveries helped to develop high-yielding plants that have added to the world's food supply.

Norman Borlaug was born in 1914, the son of Henry O. and Clara Borlaug, both immigrants from Norway. He grew up on a farm in Cresco, Iowa. Cresco and the adjoining area were known as Little Norway because almost all the residents were of Norwegian descent. As a young man, Borlaug worked hard at school and on the football field, where he was the captain of the team.

At his grandfather's urging, Borlaug enrolled at the University of Minnesota. He received a degree in forestry in 1937. After earning his doctorate, he was hired by the Du Pont Chemical Company to evaluate the effects of its fertilizers and weed killers.

A new job with the Rockefeller Foundation, however, took him to his life's work. With a team of other scientists, Borlaug went to Mexico in 1944 to investigate the possibility of developing a better strain of wheat. At this time the wheat grown in Mexico was thin-stemmed and tall. And when treated with fertilizer to increase the yield, the plants grew top-heavy and fell over.

Over the years, Borlaug mixed other wheat strains with the Mexican variety. He grew the crops in areas with different altitudes and hours of sunlight. By crossbreeding the new plants, he developed ones with great adaptability to different areas. Borlaug's improved plants were high-yielding and could be grown in areas from the equator to the 40th parallel, north and south—a region that includes the majority of the world's population.

Borlaug was working on one of his experimental plots near Mexico City in 1970 when his wife brought news that he had won the Nobel Prize. His reaction was characteristic. "That's just fine," he said, "but I still have a day's work to do here. After that we'll celebrate."

After being honored in Oslo, in the country of his ancestors, he stopped off in Cresco, Iowa. The whole town turned out to greet its famous son.

The Nobel Prize was only one of many awards Borlaug has received from governments around the world. He remains at work in Mexico today, studying and developing new seeds.

Candice Bergen

On Monday nights, millions of Americans tune in to watch Murphy Brown, TV's most amusing journalist. The program's star, Candice Bergen, is in real life very different from her character. Reserved and elegant, Bergen is the daughter of Edgar and Frances Bergen, the children of Swedish immigrants.

Edgar Bergen was a ventriloquist who began doing radio shows in the 1930s with his dummies Charlie McCarthy, Mortimer Snerd, and Effie Klinker, and later he appeared on television and in the movies. Candice recalled that as a child, she felt she had to compete with Charlie McCarthy for her father's attention.

Though her parents were wealthy, they gave Candice a small allowance and a strict upbringing. While she attended a finishing school in Switzerland, she rebelled by dyeing her hair and smoking.

As a young woman, Candice Bergen's beauty and poise won her a modeling career. She later turned to acting, making a sensational debut in the movie *The Group*. Bergen played one of several college friends whose lives take different turns after graduation. Her role in the 1971 film *Carnal Knowledge* also brought praise from critics. In 1979, she showed her talent for comedy in the movie *Starting Over*.

Bergen married Louis Malle, a French film director, and at the age of 39 became a mother. She gave up her career to raise her daughter Chloe. But she was lured back into show business after reading the script for the pilot episode of "Murphy Brown." The role was just too delightful to turn down. She said, "I love Murphy, her larger-than-lifeness, her humor, her edges. She's intolerant and impatient and crabby. She has real principles and opinions. And she doesn't suffer fools."

The show turned controversial in 1991 when Murphy Brown had a child out of wedlock. Though Vice President Dan Quayle publicly denounced the plot development, it did not hurt the show's popularity. Bergen has won several Emmy Awards for her role.

"*fjallagrös*," a sort of cure-all for bronchial troubles....

Very dear childhood memories are also associated with grandfather's sister, "*afasystir*," as I called her, who lived in a little house of two scrupulously clean rooms where there were to be seen colorful chests and other interesting objects from the far off homeland. She could recite what seem to be an endless number of ballads on many and varied subjects. There were, for example, the characters of the Nibelungenlied, Sigurd, Gudrun, the Dragon Fafnir, Brynhild, the immortal lovers Tristram and Isolde, etc. I recall her sparkling blue eyes as she warmed to her subject, sometimes reciting, sometimes singing the ballads, her trim little figure rocking back and forth, nodding her head with its shiny crop of silvery curls cut short, softly framing her delicate, alert face....

I once asked my mother what the most cherished memory was that she had of Iceland. Her reply was, "*Its silence*. Every neighborhood borders on an uninhabited area where you can retreat and become better acquainted with your soul. There your only companion is nature, unscarred and undisturbed by humanity."

Elsie Odmark came to the United States from Sweden in 1915 with five brothers and sisters to join her father and other siblings in Nebraska. Her mother died just before Elsie's 10th birthday. She remembered how her upbringing instilled a love of the Swedish heritage.

Of course, my father talked Swedish all the time, so we never heard anything but Swedish from him at home. Us children always talked Swedish to him; I did it all through my years. I left Sweden when I was so young and everybody in Sweden thought that I would not be able to remember all those things. But I give a lot of credit to the Swedish newspaper that my father got—*Svenska Amerikanaren*. I read that from the time I came over. It was printed out of Chicago and it had stories and a lot of good articles. After dad died and I got married, then we started taking it and I read up about all that was going on over in Sweden....

If I had to take my choice, I don't suppose I would want to be anything but a Swede. I always said I was very, very proud to be a Swede, because I feel this way, that the Swedish people are a very ambitious, and most of them very good, people. But I also very much love America. When I first came here, I thought it was the greatest place on earth.

In 1991, Bill and Doris Carlson, who live in Lindsborg, Kansas, described their Swedish American Christmas Eve tradition, called Dopp i Grytan.

Dopp i Grytan means "Dipping in the Pot" and that is exactly what is done during this Christmas Eve Day noon meal.

This Christmas Eve Day custom has been in the Carlson family for years. The grandparents...brought this custom with them from Värmland, Sweden in 1868....

In Sweden a kettle of broth was kept on the back of the

Sitting at a spinning wheel, Ingeborg Soderlund displays her skill at a demonstration of traditional Scandinavian handicrafts in Washington State. Behind her are many examples of folk art such as woodworking, sewing, and painted furniture.

stove throughout Christmas Eve Day. Family members would help themselves to long slices of homemade rye bread and dip it into the hot broth whenever they became hungry. This relieved the busy Mother of the household as she continued with preparations for the evening meal and the meals to be served on Christmas Day.

Since those early days here in Lindsborg, in our family the Christmas Eve *Dopp i Grytan* has become a production and a most-looked-forward-to Christmas event. Close friends are invited to share in this festive occasion and to burn their tongues right along with our family members....

No one is allowed to sit down during the meal. Following the sounding of a very loud bell and a Swedish Table Prayer, we are to line up buffet-style loading our plates with beef and pork, along with salad, herring, and extra-long slices of rye bread with butter....

Only the faint of heart and those not fully into the custom are soon out of the parade to the kettle on the stove. Others continue the parade as they remember it will be another year before we once again enjoy this quaint Swedish custom....

Finally, in the midst of the *Dopp i Grytan* meal, we always remember our parents and other family members who are no longer with us, who loved this custom so much. And also, we, as a family, recognize that other relatives are enjoying this same custom simultaneously in their own homes.

Every October, the Norsk Høstfest, the country's largest Scandinavian festival, brings thousands of people to Minot, North Dakota, to celebrate the food, folk customs, and crafts of the homeland. This craftsman demonstrates the techniques of wood carving.

A traditional Swedish celebration of St. Lucia's Day, December 13, in the IKEA furniture store in New York City. Often, the youngest daughter in a household wears the crown of candles and serves her family the traditional coffee and saffron buns known as "Lucia cats." The candles light the way in the darkness of the Swedish winter morning.

Jim Jensen, who was a TV anchorman in New York City for many years, is the son of a Danish immigrant. Jensen told interviewers about the Danish Christmas traditions that he and his family keep.

You know the kind of pastry that people call Danish? A Danish roll? That isn't what Danish pastry is like at all. It's light, flaky, extremely sweet, loaded with butter. The other "Danish" is rather heavy and dull.

Every year my wife and I send to our friends 60 *kringle,* Danish coffee cakes, from Racine, Wisconsin. That's the only place in the United States where they're made. There's a very intricate process in making them. People call Racine Kringleville. People who receive them go absolutely wild, and we tell them: "This—is Danish."...

The saying goes that at one time the Danes had conquered most of the known world, and then they withdrew and turned to cooking.

For our Christmas dinner this year we had goose stuffed with prunes and apples, mashed potatoes made with whipped cream, buttered carrots, red cabbage made from scratch with vinegar and sugar, and rice pudding. Sometimes we have a pork roast as well.

For dessert we had something that people say you have to be a born Dane to pronounce. I can't even spell it. I've heard that word all my life. My father used to try to tell me how to say it. It's made from black and red currants, grapes, raspberries, strawberries, and berries from Greenland and Iceland. It's made into a pudding. The color is a deep claret, like wine. It's brought to the table in a crystal bowl with four inches of whipped cream on top.

Berit Petersen, who lives in Bay Ridge, Brooklyn, described how she and her family keep up their Norwegian heritage.

I am a member of the Sons of Norway lodge. The Sons of Norway and other groups teach folk dancing and put on plays. We have dances and parties for Christmas and New Years Day or the 17th of May. There are still three churches whose parishioners are mostly Norwegians. Some stores sell the traditional foods. You can buy home-made *persesylte* (head cheese) and *lutefisk* and so forth.

We want to pass on the old traditions to our children. We taught our children folk dances when they were small—polkas and schottisches. The region of Norway I came from, Lindesnes, is on the far southern tip. The costumes from there are distinctive; each region has its own costume, called a *bunad*.

Our family's costumes are handmade in Norway, linen shirts, embroidered shawls. When my children were small and belonged to folk-dancing groups, they wore the costumes. My daughter has one now that she received as a college-graduation gift from my mother. They're quite expensive, because they're handmade, decorated with silver, and take a lot of work to make. Some cost as much as $10,000. I have one, and my daughter's three daughters will wear them. Right now they wear something called everyday costumes, which are less elaborate.

Inkeri Väänänen-Jensen recalled her experiences as a student in the 1970s in the Finnish program of the Scandinavian Studies Department at the University of Minnesota.

One day a student, Joyce Davis, played the *kantele*, the ancient stringed instrument of the Finns, whose origin from the bones of a pike is vividly pictured in the *Kalevala*, where it was called a fishbone harp. Joyce's *kantele* had belonged to her grandfather, John Huhtala of Bovey, Minnesota, who had come to the United States at the age of nineteen. Joyce told me that as a child, she watched her grandfather play the *kantele*, and even today, mystical, romantic memories of his early playing remain with her. In her child mind, the *kantele* seemed an enormous instrument. When her grandfather was in his late seventies, she gathered the courage to ask him if he would bequeath his *kantele* to her. He was very pleased at her request, but when she asked him to teach her how to play it, he would teach her only one chord. His fingers had stiffened with age, and he could not play the *kantele* as well as he had in previous years. He did not wish to demean his earlier playing by playing poorly now. In order to leave Joyce an instrument she could be proud of, he sent to Finland for new strings. Through the years, Joyce taught herself to play and has given a number of *kantele* performances, including some at the annual Folklife Festival in 1980 at the Smithsonian Institution in Washington, D.C.

Lauri Kahilainen, a master kantele player, during a visit to the Nordic Heritage Museum in Seattle to demonstrate his skill on the traditional Finnish stringed instrument.

Rosemaling, an art used to decorate Norwegian homes, is making a comeback in the United States. This chest is a modern example of the art.

The Anderson family, ancestors of Mardel Esping, emigrated from Sweden and settled in Axtell, Nebraska. The baby, Mabel, is Mardel's grandmother.

Mardel Esping's great grandparents, the Cederburgs, were also Swedish immigrants and Nebraska settlers. Mardel's grandfather, Gilbert, is the boy at left. He married Mabel, the girl in the photo above.

THE ESPING FAMILY

Mark and Mardel Esping are cofounders of the Folklife Institute of Central Kansas, located in Lindsborg, which has long been a center of Swedish American life. The couple's Swedish American roots date back several generations.

Q. When did your families come to the United States?

Mark:

Julius Esping arrived in 1853 with his wife, Sophia Brezelius, and their son Otto, who was three years old. Otto was my great-grandfather. They came from Döderhultan, in eastern Sweden. They were farmers and metalworkers and lived near Galesburg, Illinois.

Otto married Emma Sandburg, and they homesteaded in Kansas. Their son Oscar married Amanda Bloomberg. Their son Kenneth met Dorothy Nelson at Bethany College; they married and had three daughters and me.

My mother Dorothy's side of the family was originally from Skane. She is the result of three different Nelson families. Some were farmers. One of her great-grandfathers was a sailor who jumped ship, so he was actually an illegal immigrant. He settled in Vilas, a Swedish community in southeast Kansas. My mother's father was a carpenter, a farmer, and a banker—a very versatile man. She is still in touch with relatives that stayed in Sweden.

My father was a school administrator, first in Kansas and then in California. I started the ninth grade in Downey, California. The move depressed my father because he thought it would dissolve the family ties. However, my sisters and I came back to Kansas and married Swedish Americans. They married a Holmquist and an Elmquist.

Q: How do you account for that?

Mark:

Maybe we're just plain Midwestern people. I don't know. We all attended Bethany College in Lindsborg, where we met our spouses. The college was founded in 1881 by Lutheran Swedes and until 15 years ago was a very conservative school. It's a liberal arts college with a strong art and music emphasis.

Q: Mardel, tell us about your family background.

All eight of my great-grandparents immigrated from Sweden. My mother's grandfather Gustaf Johnson arrived in 1867, by himself. He worked for a while in Chicago till he had saved enough to bring his wife, Sarah Marie, and their four children. They lived in Bertrand, Nebraska, and then in 1887 homesteaded near Haxtun, Colorado, with a group of other Swedes. When my mother, Doris, finished high school she worked in Axtell, Nebraska, at Bethphage Mission, a Swedish Lutheran home for elderly and disabled people. My father, Winston Cederburg, was born on a farm five miles east of Axtell. He also worked at Bethphage. I have a brother, Carroll, and a sister, Karen. We grew up in North Platte, where my father worked as an engineer on the Union Pacific Railroad.

Q. What do you remember about the Swedish traditions in your family while you were growing up?

Mark:

I didn't realize that what we were doing was Swedish, because my parents didn't mention that. I don't remember being in any home that didn't have the same kind of Christmas celebration that we did. It wasn't until we moved to California that I figured out everybody wasn't the same way we were.

We attended *Julotta,* the early church service. My parents spoke Swedish when they didn't want us children to know what they were talking about. Christmas was with the grandparents; both sides fixed the traditional foods, such as *lutfisk* and *potatis korv* [potato sausage]. My mother still has an old cow horn that my father's mother gave to her. The pointed end is cut off so that it is like a funnel. You put hog guts on the small end and then push the mixture of beef, pork, and potatoes through the horn into the guts to make potato sausage.

Q: How did you feel your Swedishness growing up?

Mardel:

I would hear Swedish spoken, but I didn't learn it. I remember a children's poem called *Rida, Rida, Ranka.* We always had lingonberries and *sill* [herring], and like Mark I didn't know that those foods were not American. I just thought everybody had them. When we went to our friends' houses or church dinners, they would have *ostkaka,* which is a custard made from whole milk that's curdled using rennet. Eggs and sugar are added and it is baked.

Growing up, I didn't know that a homemaker could make white bread. I thought white bread came only from bakeries. Because my mother only made *limpa,* a brown rye, from her mother's recipe. I remember being amazed the first time she baked white bread.

Q: How did you get interested in the folklife of Swedish Americans?

Mark:

Mardel and I opened a small art gallery where we sold works by local artists. We bought an object at auction called a *Ljuskrona.* It was a paper-wrapped candelabra. We wanted to use it to decorate the front window of the gallery at Christmas. I decided to learn more about it. My uncle showed us how to cut and wrap the paper on the frame, but he didn't know any history of the object.

The Nelson family in Kansas. Mark Esping's great-grandparents are in the front row.

Otto Esping, Mark's great-grandfather, built this brown sandstone house near Lindsborg, Kansas. The distinctive stone was indigenous to the area, and builders often used it.

Oscar Esping, Mark's grandfather, operates a mule-drawn plow near Lindsborg, Kansas.

Elin Olson Nelson, Mark's great-grandmother, lived in Vilas, a Swedish enclave in southeast Kansas.

A posed carnival photograph of Mardel's mother's Aunt Lottie Johnson Axelson in an airplane model.

A friend of ours, Dr. Greta Swenson, had earned a degree in folklore at Bloomington, Indiana. We asked her to check on the *Ljuskrona*. She couldn't find anything either, so we three wrote an application for a grant from the National Endowment for the Arts. They awarded us $12,000 to study and build an exhibition about these candle holders. It was the first grant given to study a Swedish American folk art object.

The name *Ljuskrona* means "white crown." They are completely wrapped in cut paper and originally were hung from the ceiling. They were something that early immigrants made as a remembrance of Christmas in Sweden. Christmas was about the only time that immigrants took off from the drudgery of trying to wrestle a little bit of food from the prairie. They made *Ljuskrona* out of scrap materials and used the paper from packages, sacks, or even newspaper. This little bit of elegance became a symbol of hope. We even found a couple of *Ljuskrona* in nursing homes, where a person's personal possessions are very limited. That means this object has tremendous value to its owner.

Q: So that was what started the Folklife Institute?

Mark:

Yes. The three of us sat down and filled out the forms and eventually wrote another NEA grant application to examine woodworking among Swedish Americans. That grant helped us take a thousand photographs and interview woodworkers. There are still quite a few wood-carvers in the Lindsborg area. We don't have the money to make prints, so we just developed the negatives. But that means we have a record of this woodwork, which is important because things are just being lost too fast.

Q: Do you speak or teach others about these skills?

Mark:

Yes. In 1994 the Swedish Council of America invited me to speak at their biannual meeting. My topic included the idea that we should change our focus. From what makes the best Swedish smorgasbord to what makes the best Swedish-American smorgasbord.

One of the reasons I've decided to give so much time to the Folklife Institute is so maybe we can learn enough to help provide the ability for other people to redefine their heritage. For instance, most smorgasbords I attend have a Jell-O dish included, but Jell-O is not served at a "real" Swedish smorgasbord. There wasn't any Jell-O in Sweden.

As another example, my mother's *potatis korv* has more beef than when her grandmother made it. As the family rose economically, they used fewer potatoes and less pork. In Iowa, they use barley in their sausage instead of potatoes, because they grow barley there.

These adaptations are what put the hyphen in Swedish-American. I want to know what adaptations my forebears made that have allowed Swedish Americans to blend into the general society. What adaptations gave us that extra edge that allowed us as a group to do so well in America.

Mardel: I teach several Swedish American crafts. We both provide presentations for week-long Swedish Heritage Seminars sponsored by a local travel agency. I've also developed an understanding of the need for a multicultural focus in education, so I use folk arts in my public school classroom, like comparing and contrasting Scandinavian folk art painting with Hispanic folk painting.

Q: What are some of the other things the Folklife Institute has been involved in?

Mardel:

We have been collecting women's handwork. Such as lace, tatting, and costumes from Svensk Hyllningsfest, our festival. We have a storytelling project, to collect stories. That project developed from a visit to the Folklife Institute by Dr. Alan Jabbour, director of the Library of Congress Folklife Center. After spending a week in Lindsborg, he told us that the majority of the people in Lindsborg identified themselves and their place in the community through stories. So we are sponsoring a storytelling contest.

We call the contest "Lessons from the Immigrants" because that is often what they are. Some of them are very sad. One of them concerned a man who was dying in the hospital. He had had what by our standards was a horrible life. Relatives had died of diseases, his wife left him, he lost his farm—many tragedies. A friend came to see him, and when he was about to leave, they shook hands. The dying man said, "Anslut legrut," which means "the end of the grape," meaning that as far as he was concerned, life had been good. Well, that's a story that as far as I'm concerned had a real moral.

We hosted a "Folklife in the Schools" seminar for teachers and a seminar on Swedish green wood carving, *tina* box making [oval, wooden boxes], and knife making. Recently, we collected articles that were loaned to Leksand, Sweden, for an exhibition titled "More Swedish than Sweden." We also loaned wood carvings to the Döderhultan Museum in Sweden for a wood carving exhibition featuring Swedish American carvers.

The Folklife Institute owns two *Psalmodikon* we lend to young adults to learn how to play. These are early one-stringed musical instruments. We have exhibitions explaining Swedish wedding crowns and apple trees.

Mark:

We just bought a building that will be a Swedish American Cultural Center, with archives, exhibition space, and a meeting and presentation area where the results of our research may be enjoyed. Our first money-raising event to buy this building was a meal prepared by three gourmet chefs from Sweden. It was a lot of fun. That's the other thing we do, we have fun. So far it's been a lot of work that's still a lot of fun.

Mark and Mardel Esping at the Folklife Institute of Central Kansas, which they cofounded, are surrounded by the Ljuskrona that they collect and preserve.

This Kalas celebration takes place at the home of Mark's sister, Marla Elmquist. Kalas begins after Julotta (Christmas church services), at about seven o'clock in the morning and lasts until five in the afternoon. It is a whole day of eating and visiting with friends and relatives. A Ljuskrona can be seen on the table.

SCANDINAVIAN AMERICAN TIMELINE

around 1000
Leif Eriksson and his crew land in America.

1629
Jonas Bronck, a Dane, purchases land for a farm now known as the Bronx, a borough of New York City.

1638
Settlers from Sweden and Finland establish the colony of New Sweden on the Delaware River.

1776
John Morton casts the deciding vote at the Continental Congress in favor of declaring independence from Great Britain.

1825
Fifty-two Norwegians sail from Stavanger and establish the Kendall Settlement in northern New York State. It is the first large-scale Norwegian American settlement.

1841
Gustaf Unonius leads a group of settlers from Sweden to found the colony of New Uppsala near Milwaukee, Wisconsin.

1850
Jenny Lind, a renowned Swedish singer, gives a concert at Castle Garden, a theater off the tip of Manhattan. Five years later, New York State converts Castle Garden to an immigrant landing station.

1850s
Danish converts to the Church of Jesus Christ of Latter-day Saints begin migrating to Utah, where the Mormon church has its headquarters. The first Icelandic settlers also arrive in Utah around 1855.

1852
A Norwegian settlement at Bishop Hill, Illinois, is founded on land purchased by Norwegian musician Ole Bull.

1862
The *Monitor*, an ironclad warship designed by Swedish immigrant John Ericsson, engages in its first battle, against a Confederate ironclad vessel named the *Virginia*.

1862
Congress passes the Homestead Act, offering 160 acres of government land to anyone who will settle on it for five years. In the next few decades, the offer attracts many Scandinavian immigrants, most of whom settle in the northern part of the Midwest.

1862
Dania, originally an organization for all Scandinavian Americans, is founded in Chicago. It developed into a Danish American group, strongest in California.

1871
Fire destroys large areas of Chicago, and in the following years, the architect Lars G. Hallberg, a Swedish immigrant, helps design the reconstruction of the city. Many Swedish Americans find work in the construction industry of Chicago.

1882
The Danish Brotherhood in America is founded in Omaha, Nebraska.

1890
Jacob Riis publishes *How the Other Half Lives*, a study of poverty in New York City, illustrated with his photographs.

1895
The Sons of Norway, a mutual-aid society and social group, is founded in Minneapolis; it is now the largest Norwegian American organization.

1896
The Vasa Order of America, today the largest Swedish American organization, is founded in New Haven, Connecticut.

1898
Knights of Kaleva, or Finnish National Brotherhood, is founded to preserve Finnish culture in the United States.

1905
Founding of the International Workers of the World (IWW), a labor organization that sought to organize workers in all industries. Many Scandinavian Americans were active members.

1915
Carl Sandburg publishes his first book of poetry.

1919
The Icelandic National League is founded to preserve Icelandic culture in the United States.

1924-25
Ole Rölvaag's epic novel, *Giants in the Earth*, is first published in Norway. Two years later, an English translation is published in the United States.

1925
President Calvin Coolidge attends festivities in Minneapolis for the celebration of 100 years of Norwegian immigration.

1927
Gutzon Borglum begins work on the Mount Rushmore National Monument.

1927
Charles A. Lindbergh becomes the first person to fly across the Atlantic Ocean alone.

1932
"Babe" Didrikson Zaharias wins two gold medals at the Olympic games, the beginning of her career as the foremost woman athlete in the United States.

1938
Chester Carlson develops the copying process that he called xerography; he later licensed the commercial rights to a company that became the Xerox Corporation.

1953
Earl Warren is named chief justice of the United States.

1970
Norman Borlaug wins the Nobel Peace Prize for his scientific contributions to the green revolution.

1996
Celebration of the sesquicentennial of the beginning of mass emigration from Sweden. The king and queen of Sweden attend the festivities at Ellis Island.

FURTHER READING

General Accounts of Scandinavian American History

Blegen, Theodore C. *Norwegian Migration to America.* New York: Haskell House, 1969.

Carlsson, Sten. *Swedes in North America, 1638–1988.* Stockholm: Streiffert, 1988.

Hale, Frederick, ed. *Danes in North America.* Seattle: University of Washington Press, 1984.

Haugen, Einar. *The Norwegians in America, 1825–1975.* New York: Norwegian Information Service, 1976.

Hoglund, A. William. *Finnish Immigrants in America, 1880–1920.* Madison: University of Wisconsin Press, 1960.

Larsen, Birgit Flemming, and Henning Bender, eds. *Danish Emigration to the U.S.A.* Aalborg, Denmark: Danes Worldwide Archives and Danish Society for Emigration History, 1992.

Lovoll, Odd S. *The Promise of America: A History of the Norwegian-American People.* Minneapolis: University of Minnesota Press in cooperation with the Norwegian-American Historical Association, 1984.

Moberg, Vilhelm. *The Unknown Swedes.* Translated and edited by Roger McKnight. Carbondale: Southern Illinois University Press, 1988.

Semmingsen, Ingrid. *Norway to America: A History of the Migration.* Translated by Einar Haugen. Minneapolis: University of Minnesota Press, 1978.

Sherman, William C., et al. *Plains Folk: North Dakota's Ethnic History.* Fargo: North Dakota Institute for Regional Studies, 1988.

Veirs, Kristina, ed. *Nordic Heritage Northwest.* With photographs by Scotty Sapiro and text by Nancy Hausauer. Seattle: The Writing Works in association with the Nordic Heritage Museum, 1982.

Walters, Thorstina. *Modern Sagas: The Story of the Icelanders in North America.* Fargo: North Dakota Institute for Regional Studies, 1953.

Wagner, Sally Roesch, ed. *Daughters of Dakota.* Aberdeen, S. Dak.: Sky Carrier Press, 1989, 1991.

Wudrinenen, John H. *The Finns on the Delaware: 1638–1655.* New York: AMS Press, 1966.

Personal Accounts of Scandinavian American Life

Barton, H. Arnold, ed. *Letters from the Promised Land: Swedes in America, 1840–1914.* Minneapolis: University of Minnesota Press for the Swedish Pioneer Society, 1975.

Cain, Betty Swanson. *American from Sweden: the Story of A. V. Swanson.* Carbondale: Southern Illinois University Press, 1987.

Engelmann, Ruth. *Leaf House: Days of Remembering.* New York: Harper & Row, 1982.

Farseth, Pauline, and Theodore C. Blegen, trans. & eds. *Frontier Mother: The Letters of Gro Svendsen.* New York: Arno Press, 1979.

Hannula, Reino Nikolai. *Blueberry God: The Education of a Finnish-American.* San Luis Obispo, Calif.: Quality Hill Books, 1990.

Jarvenpa, Aili, ed. *In Two Cultures: The Stories of Second Generation Finnish-Americans.* St. Cloud, Minn.: North Star Press of St. Cloud, 1992.

Jarvenpa, Aili, and Michael G. Karni, eds. *Sampo, The Magic Mill.* Minneapolis: New Rivers Press, 1989.

Larson, Laurence M. *The Log Book of a Young Immigrant.* Northfield, Minn.: Norwegian-American Historical Association, 1939.

Lindbergh, Charles A. *Autobiography of Values.* New York: Harcourt Brace Jovanovich, 1978.

Morrison, Joan, and Charlotte Fox Zabusky. *American Mosaic: The Immigrant Experience in the Words of Those Who Lived It.* Pittsburgh: University of Pittsburgh Press, 1980.

Olsson, Anna. *A Child of the Prairie.* Translated by Martha Winblad and edited by Elizabeth Jaderborg. Lindsborg, Kans.: Folklife Institute of Central Kansas, 1978.

Osland, Birger. *A Long Pull from Stavanger.* Northfield, Minn.: Norwegian-American Historical Association, 1945.

Polvi, Isaac. *The Autobiography of a Finnish Immigrant.* Edited by Joseph Damrell. St. Cloud, Minn.: North Star Press of St. Cloud, 1991.

Raaen, Aagot. *Grass of the Earth: Immigrant Life in the Dakota Country.* New York: Arno Press, 1979.

Rasmussen, Janet, ed. *New Land, New Lives: Scandinavian Immigrants to the Pacific Northwest.* Seattle: University of Washington Press, 1993.

Riis, Jacob A. *The Making of an American.* Edited by Roy Lubove. New York: Harper & Row, 1966.

Stilling, Niels Peter, and Anne Lisbeth Olsen. *A New Life: Danish Emigration to North America as Described by the Emigrants Themselves in Letters, 1842–1946.* Translated by Karen Veien. Aalborg, Denmark: Danes Worldwide Archives in collaboration with the Danish Society for Emigration History, 1994.

Väänänen-Jensen, Inkeri. *My Story: Inkeri's Journey.* Iowa City: Penfield Press, 1994.

Warren, Earl. *The Memoirs of Earl Warren.* Garden City, N.Y.: Doubleday, 1977.

Zempel, Solveig, ed. *In Their Own Words: Letters from Norwegian Immigrants.* Minneapolis: University of Minnesota Press in cooperation with the Norwegian-American Historical Association, 1991.

TEXT CREDITS

Main Text

p. 12, top: Jacob Riis, *The Making of an American,* ed. Roy Lubove (New York: Harper & Row, 1966), 12-13, 16-18.

p. 12, bottom: Sally Roesch Wagner, ed., *Daughters of Dakota,* vol. 1 (Aberdeen, S. Dak.: Sky Carrier Press, 1989), 7-8.

p. 13, top: Thorstina Walters, *Modern Sagas: The Story of the Icelanders in North America* (Fargo: North Dakota Institute for Regional Studies, 1953), 9-10.

p. 13, bottom: Hamilton Holt, ed., *The Life Stories of Undistinguished Americans as Told by Themselves* (New York: Routledge, 1990), 49-50.

p. 14: Isaac Polvi, *The Autobiography of a Finnish-American Immigrant,* ed. Joseph Damrell (St. Cloud, Minn.: North Star Press of St. Cloud), 13-14.

p. 15: Janet Rasmussen, ed., *New Land, New Lives: Scandinavian Immigrants to the Pacific Northwest* (Seattle: University of Washington Press, 1993), 21-23.

p. 16: Rasmussen, *New Land, New Lives,* 21-23.

p. 17: Rasmussen, *New Land, New Lives,* 36-39.

p. 18, top: Wagner, *Daughters of Dakota,* vol. 4 (Aberdeen, S.Dak.: Sky Carrier Press, 1991), 159.

p. 18, bottom: Stilling, N. P. "Letter from America." In Birgit Flemming Larsen and Henning Bender, eds., *Danish Emigration to the U.S.A.* (Aalborg, Denmark: Danes Worldwide Archives , 1992), 34. Originally published in Olsen, A. L., Stilling, N. P., *Et Nyt Liv. Den danske udvandring til Nordamerika i billeder og breve* [A New Life. Danish Emigration to North America in Pictures and Letters]. Copenhagen: Strandbergs Forlag, 1985, p. 25.

p. 19: Holt, *Life Stories,* 50-51.

p. 20, top: Ingrid Semmingsen, *Norway to America: A History of the Migration,* trans. Einar Haugen (Minneapolis: University of Minnesota Press, 1978), 167.

p. 20, bottom: Rasmussen, *New Land, New Lives,* 299-300.

p. 21, top: Reprinted from *American Mosaic: The American Experience in the Words of Those Who Lived It,* by Joan Morrison and Charlotte Fox Zabusky, by permission of the University of Pittsburgh Press © 1980, 1993 by Joan Morrison and Charlotte Fox Zabusky, page 5.

p. 21, middle: Polvi, *Autobiography,* 14.

p. 21, bottom: Rasmussen, *New Land, New Lives,* 196-97.

p. 26, top: H. Arnold Barton, ed., *Letters from the Promised Land: Swedes in America, 1840–1914* (Minneapolis: University of Minnesota Press, 1975), 53.

p. 26, bottom: Barton, *Letters,* 121-23.

p. 27: Niels Peter Stilling and Anne Lisbeth Olsen, *A New Life: Danish Emigration to North America as Described by the Emigrants Themselves in Letters, 1842–1946.* Translated from the Danish by Karen Veien. (Aalborg, Denmark: Danes Worldwide Archives, 1994), pp. 53-54 (Danes Worldwide Archives Studies in Emigration History, no. 6), originally published in Stilling, N. P., "Fiskerfamilien ved Michigan-søen" [The Fishing Family at Lake Michigan]. In Hansen, M. H.; Vestergaard, B.; Jørgensen, S. E.; Olsen, A. L.; Stilling, N. P., eds. *Brev fra Amerika. Danske Udvandrerbreve 1874–1922* [Letter from America. Danish Emigrant Letters 1874–1922]. Copenhagen: Gyldendal, 1981, pp. 307-10.

p. 28, top: Jeffrey A. Hess, *Three Immigrant Stories* (St. Paul: Minnesota Historical Society, 1977), 26-27. Copyright © 1977 by the Minnesota Historical Society.

p. 28, bottom: Rasmussen, *New Land, New Lives,* 24-25.

p. 29: Riis, *The Making of an American,* 33-34.

p. 30, top: Frederick Hale, ed., *Danes in North America* (Seattle: University of Washington Press, 1984), 8-9.

p. 30, bottom: Birger Osland, *A Long Pull from Stavanger* (Northfield, Minn.: Norwegian-American Historical Association, 1945), 8.

p. 31, top: Stilling and Olsen, *A New Life: Danish Emigration to North America,* 52. Originally published in: Olsen, A. L., and Stilling, N. P. *Et Nyt Liv. Den danske udvandring til Nordamerika i billeder og breve* [A New Life. Danish Emigration to North America in Pictures and Letters]. Copenhagen: Strandbergs Forlag, 1985, p. 45.

p. 31, bottom: Rasmussen, *New Land, New Lives,* 143.

p. 32, top: John H. Wuorinen, *The Finns on the Delaware 1638–1655* (New York: AMS Press, 1966), 67-68.

p. 32, bottom: Adolph B. Benson and Naboth Hedin, *Americans from Sweden* (Philadelphia: Lippincott, 1950), 86-87.

p. 33, top: Jehu Curtis Clay, *Annals of the Swedes on the Delaware* (Chicago: John Ericsson Memorial Committee, 1938), 86-87.

p. 33, bottom: Adolph B. Benson, ed., *Peter Kalm's Travels in North America,* vol. 2 (New York: Wilson-Erickson, 1937), 683.

p. 36, top: Polvi, *Autobiography,* 127.

p. 36, bottom: Henrietta Larson, ed. and trans., "The Sinking of the *Atlantic* on Lake Erie. An Immigrant Journey from Quebec to Wisconsin in 1852," in *Norwegian-American Studies and Records,* vol. 4 (Northfield, Minn.: Norwegian-American Historical Association, 1929), 996-98.

p. 37: Howard Shaff and Audrey Karl Shaff, *Six Wars At a Time* (Sioux Falls, S. Dak.: Center for Western Studies at Augustana College in cooperation with Permelia Publishing, 1985), 11.

p. 38, top: Reprinted from *American Mosaic: The American Experience in the Words of Those Who Lived It,* by Joan Morrison and Charlotte Fox Zabusky, by permission of the University of Pittsburgh Press © 1980, 1993 by Joan Morrison and Charlotte Fox Zabusky, page 37.

p. 38, bottom: Barton, *Letters,* 277.

p. 39: Hess, *Three Immigrant Stories,* 27. Copyright © 1977 by the Minnesota Historical Society.

p. 40, top: Arne Odd Johnsen, "Johannes Nordboe and Norwegian Immigration," in *Norwegian-American Studies and Records,* Vol. 8 (Northfield, Minn.: Norwegian-American Historical Association, 1934), 24-25.

p. 40, bottom: Cathy Luchetti, *Home on the Range: A Culinary History of the American West* (New York: Villard, 1993), 137-38.

p. 41, top: Riis, *The Making of an American,* 38-39.

p. 41, bottom: Walters, *Modern Sagas,* 11-12.

p. 42, top: Barton, *Letters,* 143.

p. 42, bottom: Holt, *Life Stories,* 59.

p. 43, top: Aarre Lahti, "I Grew Up in Ironwood," *Finn Heritage* (San Luis Obispo, Calif.) 4, no. 4 (Summer 1989): 23.

p. 43, middle: Rasmussen, *New Land, New Lives,* 60.

p. 43, bottom: Barton, *Letters,* 267.

p. 48, top: Hale, *Danes in North America,* 98-99.

p. 48, middle: Aili Jarvenpa, ed., *In Two Cultures: The Stories of Second-Generation Finnish-Americans* (St. Cloud, Minn.: North Star Press of St. Cloud, 1992), 107.

p. 48, bottom: Charles A. Lindbergh, "A Farm Boy Dreams," in *America Remembers,* ed. Samuel Rapport and Patricia Schartle (Garden City, N.Y.: Hanover House, 1956), 173-74.

p. 49: Alice Lynd and Staughton Lynd, eds., *Rank and File: Personal Histories of Working-Class Organizers* (Boston: Beacon Press, 1973), 37-38.

p. 50, top: Reprinted from *American Mosaic: The American Experience in the Words of Those Who Lived It,* by Joan Morrison and Charlotte Fox Zabusky, by permission of the University of Pittsburgh Press © 1980, 1993 by Joan Morrison and Charlotte Fox Zabusky, pp. 38-39.

p. 50, bottom: Cecyle S. Neidle, *The New Americans* (New York: Twayne, 1967), 208.

p. 51, top: Thorstina Jackson, "Icelandic Communities in America: Cultural Backgrounds and Early Settlements," in *Norwegian-American Studies and Records,* vol. 3 (Northfield, Minn.: Norwegian-American Historical Association, 1928), 110.

p. 51, bottom: Rasmussen, *New Land, New Lives,* 178.

p. 52, top: Rasmussen, *New Land, New Lives,* 215-16.

p. 52, bottom: Rasmussen, *New Land, New Lives,* 150.

p. 54, top: Hale, *Danes in North America,* 60-61.

p. 54, bottom: Barton, *Letters,* 127.

p. 55: Riis, *The Making of an American,* 44-46.

p. 56: Polvi, *Autobiography,* 133-35.

p. 57: Reprinted from *American Mosaic: The American Experience in the Words of Those Who Lived It,* by Joan Morrison and Charlotte Fox Zabusky, by permission of the University of Pittsburgh Press © 1980, 1993 by Joan Morrison and Charlotte Fox Zabusky, pp. 25-26.

p. 58, top: Theodore C. Blegen, "Immigrant Women and the American Frontier: Three Early 'America Letters,'" in *Norwegian-American Studies and Records,* vol. 5 (Northfield, Minn.: Norwegian-American Historical Association, 1930), 18-22.

p. 58, bottom: Stilling and Olsen, *A New Life: Danish Emigration to North America,* 124-25. Originally published in: Olsen, A. L., and Stilling, N. P. *Et Nyt Liv. Den danske udvandring til Nordamerika i billeder og breve* [A New Life. Danish Emigration to North America in Pictures and Letters]. Copenhagen: Strandbergs Forlag, 1985, pp. 106-7.

p. 59: Reprinted from *American Mosaic: The American Experience in the Words of Those Who Lived It,* by Joan Morrison and Charlotte Fox Zabusky, by permission of the University of Pittsburgh Press © 1980, 1993 by Joan Morrison and Charlotte Fox Zabusky, pp. 16-17.

p. 60, top: Jeff Kisseloff, *You Must Remember This: An Oral History of Manhattan from the 1890s to World War II* (San Diego: Harcourt Brace Jovanovich, 1989), 398-99.

p. 60, bottom: Velma Antilla Koven, "I Grew Up In a Finnish Boardinghouse," *Finn Heritage* (San Luis Obispo, Calif.) 5, no. 4 (Summer 1990): 17-19.

p. 62, top: Hale, *Danes in North America,* 26-27.

p. 62, bottom: Holt, *Life Stories,* 53, 56-57, 58.

p. 64, top: Allan O. Kownslar, *The Texans: Their Land and History* (New York: American Heritage, 1972), 288-89.

p. 64, bottom: Barton, *Letters,* 185.

p. 65, top: Pauline Farseth and Theodore C. Blegen, trans. and eds., *Frontier Mother: The Letters of Gro Svendsen* (New York: Arno Press, 1979), 40.

p. 65, bottom: Barton, *Letters,* 154.

p. 66, top: Charles Vandersluis, comp. and ed., *Ninety Years at St. Paul's* (Marshall, Minn.: Ousman, 1977), 16-17.

p. 66, bottom: Stilling and Olsen, *A New Life: Danish Emigration to North America,* 147-48. Originally published in: Olsen, A. L. "Farmertilvaerelsen i Californien og Texas" [The Life as a Farmer in California and Texas]. In Hansen, M. H.; Vestergaard, B.; Jørgensen, S. E.; Olsen, A. L.; Stilling, N. P., eds. *Brev fra Amerika. Danske Udvandrerbreve 1874–1922* [Letter from America. Danish Emigrant Letters 1874–1922]. Copenhagen: Gyldendal, 1981, p. 229.

p. 67: Jarvenpa, *In Two Cultures,* 5, 6-7.

p. 68: Walters, *Modern Sagas,* 1-2.

p. 69, top: Wagner, *Daughters of Dakota,* vol. 4, 130.

p. 69, bottom: Laurence M. Larson, *The Log Book of A Young Immigrant* (Northfield, Minn.: Norwegian-American Historical Association, 1939), 32-33.

p. 70, top: Ellen R. Larson, "Our Heritage," author's typescript, pp. 18-19.

p. 70, bottom: Mrs. R. O. Brandt, "Social Aspects of Prairie Pioneering: The Reminiscences of a Pioneer Pastor's Wife," in *Norwegian-American Studies and Records,* vol. 7 (Northfield, Minn.: Norwegian-American Historical Association, 1933), 5-6.

p. 71: Reprinted from *American Mosaic: The American Experience in the Words of Those Who Lived It,* by Joan Morrison and Charlotte Fox Zabusky, by permission of the University of Pittsburgh Press © 1980, 1993 by Joan Morrison and Charlotte Fox Zabusky, page 16.

p. 72, top: Stilling and Olsen, *A New Life: Danish Emigration to North America,* 130-31. Originally published in: Olsen, A. L., and Stilling, N. P. *Et Nyt Liv. Den danske udvandring til Nordamerika i billeder og breve* [A New Life. Danish Emigration to North America in Pictures and Letters]. Copenhagen: Strandbergs Forlag, 1985, p. 111.

p. 72, bottom: Barton, *Letters,* 227.

p. 73: Barton, *Letters,* 218.

p. 74, top: Lynd, *Rank and File,* 43.

p. 74, bottom: Weidle, *The New Americans,* 208.

p. 75: Reino Nikolai Hannula, *Blueberry God: The Education of a Finnish-American* (San Luis Obispo, Calif.: Quality Hill Books, 1990), 130-31.

p. 80: Aagot Raaen, *Grass of the Earth: Immigrant Life in the Dakota Country* (New York: Arno Press, 1979), 112-13.

p. 81, top: Betty Swanson Cain, *American from Sweden: The Story of A. V. Swanson* (Carbondale: Southern Illinois University Press, 1987), 59-61.

p. 81, bottom: Lahti, "I Grew Up in Ironwood," 24.

p. 82: Inkeri Väänänen-Jensen, *My Story, Inkeri's Journey* (Iowa City: Penfield Press, 1994), 60-61.

p. 83, top: Stilling and Olsen, *A New Life: Danish Emigration to North America,* 155-56, 174. Originally published in: Olsen, A. L., and Stilling, N. P. *Et Nyt Liv. Den danske udvandring til Nordamerika i billeder og breve* [A New Life. Danish Emigration to North America in Pictures and Letters]. Copenhagen: Strandbergs Forlag, 1985, pp. 134-35, 153.

p. 83, bottom: Jackson, "Icelandic Communities in America," 111.

p. 84, top: Barton, *Letters,* 230.

p. 84, bottom: Rasmussen, *New Land, New Lives,* 188.

p. 85, top: Barton, *Letters,* 168-69.

p. 85, bottom: Hale, *Danes in North America*, 95-96.

p. 86: Solveig Zempel, ed., *In Their Own Words: Letters from Norwegian Immigrants* (Minneapolis: University of Minnesota Press in cooperation with the Norwegian-American Historical Association, 1991), 178-79.

p. 87, top: Myrna Katz Frommer and Harvey Frommer, *It Happened in Brooklyn: An Oral History* (New York: Harcourt Brace, 1993), 89-90, 98, 133.

p. 87, bottom: personal interview, December 25, 1995.

p. 88: personal interview, December 27, 1995.

p. 89: Hess, *Three Immigrant Stories*, 29-30. Copyright © 1977 by the Minnesota Historical Society.

p. 90, top: Barton, *Letters*, 265-66.

p. 90, bottom: Stilling and Olsen, *A New Life: Danish Emigration to North America*, 144. Originally published in: Olsen, A. L., and Stilling, N. P. *Et Nyt Liv. Den danske udvandring til Nordamerika i billeder og breve* [A New Life. Danish Emigration to North America in Pictures and Letters]. Copenhagen: Strandbergs Forlag, 1985, p. 124-25. The letters of Natalie Bering first appeared in: Larsen, K. *De, Der Tog Hjemmefra* [Those Who Left Home], vol. 2, Copenhagen: Nordisk Forlag, 1912.

p. 91: Walters, *Modern Sagas*, 3, 5-6.

p. 92: Wagner, *Daughters of Dakota*, vol. 4, 126-27, 128-29.

p. 93, top: Reprinted from *American Mosaic: The American Experience in the Words of Those Who Lived It*, by Joan Morrison and Charlotte Fox Zabusky, by permission of the University of Pittsburgh Press © 1980, 1993 by Joan Morrison and Charlotte Fox Zabusky, pp. 27-28.

p. 93, bottom: Babe Didrikson Zaharias, as told to Harry Paxton, *This Life I've Led* (New York: Barnes, 1955), 7-9.

p. 94: Lynd, *Rank and File*, 38-39.

p. 95: Ruth Engelmann, *Leaf House: Days of Remembering* (New York: Harper & Row, 1982), 59-61.

p. 96, top: Zempel, *In Their Own Words*, 11-12.

p. 96, bottom: Wagner, *Daughters of Dakota*, vol. 4, 129-30.

p. 97, top: Lynd, *Rank and File*, 40.

p. 97, bottom: Wayne Charles Miller, *A Handbook of American Minorities* (New York: New York University Press, 1976), 135, 137-38.

p. 98: Jarvenda, *In Two Cultures*, 47.

p. 99: Engelmann, *Leaf House*, 50-51.

p. 100: Stilling and Olsen, *A New Life: Danish Emigration to North America*, 26-27.

p. 101: Larson, *The Log Book of a Young Immigrant*, 131, 132-34.

p. 102, top: Barton, *Letters*, 172.

p. 102, bottom: Bak, A. A. "The Importance of Images. Thorvaldsen, Dorph and Other Artists in Danish-American Churches." In Birgit Flemming Larsen and Henning Bender, eds., *Danish Emigration to the U.S.A.* (Aalborg, Denmark: Danes Worldwide Archives, 1992), 101. Originally published in Nielsen, Karma J., *St. Ansgar's Lutheran Church, 1880–1980*. (Salinas, Calif.: St. Ansgar's Lutheran Church, 1980), 20.

p. 103: Aili Jarvenpa and Michael G. Karni, eds., *Sampo, the Magic Mill* (Minneapolis: New Rivers Press, 1989), 325.

p. 108: Barton, *Letters*, 258-59.

p. 109: Earl Warren, *The Memoirs of Earl Warren* (Garden City, N.Y.: Doubleday, 1977), 265-67.

p. 110, top: Rasmussen, *New Land, New Lives*, 297.

p. 110, middle: Rasmussen, *New Land, New Lives*, 25.

p. 110, bottom: Jarvenda, *In Two Cultures*, 32-33.

p. 111, top: Jarvenda, *In Two Cultures*, 57, 60.

p. 111, bottom: Stilling and Olsen, *A New Life: Danish Emigration to North America*, 199. Originally published in: Olsen, A. L., and Stilling, N. P. *Et Nyt Liv. Den danske udvandring til Nordamerika i billeder og breve* [A New Life. Danish Emigration to North America in Pictures and Letters]. Copenhagen: Strandbergs Forlag, 1985, p. 174.

p. 112, top: Rasmussen, *New Land, New Lives*, 297-98.

p. 112, bottom: Rasmussen, *New Land, New Lives*, 279-80.

p. 113: Walters, *Modern Sagas*, 7-8, 10, 16-17.

p. 114, top: Rasmussen, *New Land, New Lives*, 114-15.

p. 114, bottom: Bill Carlson and Doris Carlson, *Svensk Hyllingsfest* (Lindsborg, Kans.: Folklife Institute of Central Kansas, 1991), 44.

p. 116, top: personal interview, December 27, 1995.

p. 116, bottom: personal interview, June 12, 1996.

p. 117: Väänänen-Jensen, *My Story*, 155-56.

Sidebars

p. 21: H. Arnold Barton, ed., *Letters from the Promised Land: Swedes in America, 1840–1914* (Minneapolis: University of Minnesota Press, 1975), 256.

p. 28: first song: Barton, *Letters*, 34; second song: Arlow W. Andersen, *The Norwegian-Americans* (Boston: Twayne, 1975), 24; third song: Sakari Sariola, "Köyhän Mamman Lapsia," *Finn Heritage* (San Luis Obispo, Calif.) 5, no. 1 (Fall 1989): 7.

p. 37: Theodore C. Blegen, *Norwegian Migration to America, 1825–1860* (New York: Haskell House, 1969), 117.

p. 39: Blegen, *Norwegian Migration*, 344.

p. 52: Kristina Veirs, ed., *Nordic Heritage Northwest* (Seattle: Nordic Heritage Museum, The Writing Works, 1982), 28-29.

p. 57: Matti Pelto, "Memories from the Minnesota Iron Ore Mines," trans. Vienna C. Maki, in *The Best of Finnish American*, ed. Michael G. Kaenc, © copyright Finnish American Publications (Iowa City: Penfield Press, 1994), 40.

p. 58: Roger Daniels, *Coming to America* (New York: HarperCollins, 1990), 169.

p. 74: quoted material from Wayne Charles Miller, *A Handbook of American Minorities* (New York: New York University Press, 1976), 17-18.

p. 93: Thorstina Walters, *Modern Sagas: The Story of the Icelanders in North America* (Fargo: North Dakota Institute for Regional Studies, 1953), 146.

p. 99: Aagot Raaen, *Grass of the Earth: Immigrant Life in the Dakota Country* (New York: Arno Press, 1979), 85.

PICTURE CREDITS

Archives of Labor and Urban Affairs, Wayne State University: 75 bottom; Arizona Historical Society: 74 (#43172); Bishop Hill Historical Association: 43; Solomon D. Butcher Collection, Nebraska State Historical Society: 69 top; Bystrom Family Collection: 12, 16 top, 81 bottom; © Martha Cooper, City Lore: 107; The Danish Immigrant Museum, an International Culture Center: cover, 25, 92 top, 97 bottom; Delaware Swedish Colonial Society, Dr. V. Eugene McCoy: 32; Velma Doby: 50; 1877 Peterson Station Museum, Peterson, Minn.: 55 bottom; Mark and Mardel Esping: 118-21; Fenton Historical Society: 71 top, 72 top; Nelson Gerrard, Eyrarbakki Icelandic Heritage and Genealogical Centre, Arborg, Manitoba, Canada: 91 top; courtesy of the Goodhue County Historical Society, Red Wing, Minn.: 87 bottom; Ida Gurney: 90 bottom; Joann Laitinen Hall: 57 bottom; Helen Lahtinen Hannula: 58; Reino Hannula: 33; Hedmarksmuseet og Domkirkeodden: 30, 48, 62 top, 98 bottom, 108 bottom; Henry Hirvi: 111; Thomas Hoobler: 108 top, 116 bottom; Fred Hultstrand History in Pictures Collection, NDIRS-NDSU, Fargo, N. Dak.: 44, 65, 80, 91 bottom, 97 top; courtesy of Hubert H. Humphrey III: 6, 7 bottom; The Humphrey Forum, University of Minnesota: 7 middle; Immigrant History Research Center: 53 bottom, 57 top, 78, 82, 84 bottom, 87 top, 88 top, 95 bottom; Institute of Texan Cultures, San Antonio, Tex.: 83 bottom (Mr. & Mrs. Clarence Colwick); 94 bottom (Hansen Collection); Leola Josefson and Sharlotte Anderson Mendenhall: 85 bottom; Kansas State Historical Society: 39, 92 bottom, 121 top; Library of Congress: 26, 34; Ljósmyndasafn Reykjavíkur: 14 top, 15 bottom; Lokalhistorisk Arkiv for Aalborg Kommune: 73 top, 98 top; Milwaukee Public Museum: 38 top; Minnesota Historical Society: frontispiece (Joseph Paulicek), 7 top, 22, 38 bottom (Poster Collection), 42, 59 top (Straus), 61 top (Metropolitan Medical Center, photo by Eggen), 63, 72 bottom, 76 (photo by S. C. Sargent, Taylors Falls), 81 top, 83 top, 93 (*St. Paul Daily News*); MTU Archives and Copper Country Historical Collections, Michigan Technological University: 54 bottom (#01285-Donor: Nils Eilertsen), 68 (#04002-Donor: Patricia Ex), 75 top (#01486-Donor: Tony Vranesich), 96; Museum of History and Industry, Seattle, Wash.: 49 bottom; National Museum of Denmark: 14 bottom; National Museum of Finland: 8, 16 bottom; courtesy National Park Service, Mount Rushmore National Memorial: 66; New York Public Library of the Performing Arts: 110; New York Public Library Picture Collection: 86; Nordic Heritage Museum, Seattle, Wash.: 17 bottom, 27 bottom, 47, 53 top right, 71 bottom, 100 top, 104; Norsk Folkemuseum: 10, 27 bottom; Norsk Høstfest Association, Minot, N. Dak.: 18, 21; Eija Pulli Nvotio and Nancy Austin: 20; Ohlinger: 114; Oregon Historical Society #CN010735: 56; Pacific Lutheran University: 11, 15 top, 31 bottom, 89; Berit Petersen: 17 top; Holger Munchaus Petersen: 36; Royal Library, Copenhagen: 19, 29 bottom; Runestone Museum, Alexandria, Minn.: 109; courtesy San Francisco Maritime National Historic Park: 5 (P50-36,617), 51 bottom (P77-040a, #12); Photography: Scotty Sapiro: 117 top; Seattle Post-Intelligencer Collection, Museum of History and Industry: 61 bottom, 115; Solvang (Calif.) Conference and Visitors Bureau: 112; Sovittaja Archives: 29 top; State Historical Society of North Dakota: 79, 102; State Historical Society of Wisconsin: 37 (WHi X3-50620), 64 (WHi X3-50625), 67 (WHi 50619), 100 bottom (WHi X3-50622); Statsarkivet i Stavanger: 13; Laila Suomela: 69 bottom; Swenson Swedish Immigration History Center: 46; Elsie Tenney: 41; Trinity Lutheran Church, Worcester, Mass.: 101; Oiva Tuomi: 59 bottom; Jim Turner: 106; Special Collections Division, University of Washington Libraries: 49 top (photo by Darius Kinsey, negative no. 155A), 53 middle (negative no. U.W.#12221), 53 top left (photo by Wilse, negative no. 1209), 54 top (photo by E. A. Hegg, negative no. 778), 55 top (photo by Larss & Duclos, negative no. 1); Utah State Historical Society: 60, 94 top; Vesterheim Norwegian-American Museum: 24, 31 top, 51 top, 62 bottom, 70, 84 top, 95 top, 103, 113, 117 bottom; Kirk Wiebe: 90 top; courtesy of Neal D. and Ferne Larson Williams of Lincoln, Nebr.: 40; Worcester (Mass.) Historical Museum: 85 top.

INDEX

Page numbers in *italics* indicate illustrations.

Actors, 106
Ager, Waldemer, 105
Ahl, William, 48
Aldous, Christiane, 37
Althing (Icelandic parliament), 10, 11
America fever, 11, 18-21
America letters, 18, 24, 32-33
Anaconda Mining Company, 47
Andersen, Annette, 35
Andersen, Ole, 45
Anderson, Charles T., 35
Anderson, Hilma Swenson, *22*
Anderson, John B., 107
Anderson, John W., 49-50, 74, 94-95, 97
Anderson, Mary, 50-51, 74
Anderson, Olafur G., *85*
Andrén, August, *54-55*
Ann-Margret, 106
Architects, 46-47, 105
Arnesen, Bob, 87
Aroostook County, Maine, 46
Artists, 106
Aslakson, Aase, *12-13*
Astoria, Oreg., *53*
Athletes, 93-94, 105-6

Bakken, Orville, *108*
Beckof, Christian, 102-3
Belin, Hulda, 43
Bendix, Vincent, 105
Bergen, Candice, 106, *114*
Bergen, Edgar, 106, 114
Berglund, Marie Torheim, 84-85
Bergman, Fredrik, 64-65
Bering, Natalie, 90-91
Bisbee, Ariz., strike, *56, 74*
Bishop Hill, Ill., *43*
Björk, Eric, 33
Blindheim, Ole, 35
Borg, George Norman, 105
Borglum, Gutzon, 66, 106
Borglum, Lincoln, 66, 106
Borlaug, Norman, *113*
Bremer, Frederika, 39
Bronck, Jonas, 23
Bronx, N.Y., 23
Brooklyn, N.Y., 77-78, *81,* 87-88, *108,*
    116-17
Building trades, 46
Business owners, 105
*Bygdelags (*Norwegian American clubs),
    79

Cain, Betty Swanson, 81
Carlson, Bill and Doris, 114-15
Carlson, Chester, 105
Carter, Kate Bearnson, 107
Castle Garden, 35
Chicago, Ill., 46-47, 77, 85-86
Choral groups, 78, 79, *83,* 112
Christiansen, Henrich, 23
Christmas, 15, 40-41, 88, *92,* 114-15,
    116, 119, *121*
Church of Jesus Christ of Latter-day
    Saints. *See* Mormons
Citizenship, 47

Civil War (U.S.), 45-46
Colleges, 79, 118
Colonial settlers, 23, 24, *32-33*
Communities, 23, *32,* 39, *43,* 45, 46,
    55, 71, 72, 73, 77-79, 80-89, 92, 103,
    107, *112*
Confirmation, 17, *101-2*
Continental Congress, 23, 33
Cooperative stores, 78, *84*
Crookhorn, Evelyn, 60

Dairy industry, *14,* 45, 66-67
Danevang, Tex., *94*
Danielson, John Peter, 72
Danish Brotherhood, 79, 88
Danish Constitution Day, 107
Daughters of Norway, 85
Decorah, Iowa, 81, *84*
Dickerson, Inga Hansen, 18
Doby, Velma Hakkila, 111
Domestic servants, 46, *58,* 60
Dopp i Grytan, 114-15

Eddas, 10
Ellington, Karl-Johan, 73
Ellis Island, 35, *37,* 39
Emigrant guidebooks, 24-25, 35
Emigrant societies, 24
Engelmann, Ruth, *95,* 99
Eric, King (of Denmark), 11
Ericsson, John, 45-46
Eriksson, Leif. *See* Leif Eriksson
Erik the Red, *9-10*
Esping family, *118-21*
Ethölén, Arvid A., 25
Explorers, 9-10, 105

Factories, 46, *72-75*
Fahl, Hans, 31
Family, *90-95*
Farming, *15,* 16, 17, 45-46, *62-71,* 93,
    94-95
FinnFest, 107
Finn halls, 78, 81-82, 89
Finnish Brotherhood, 79
Fishing, *17,* 46-47, *51-53*
Fitchburg, Mass., 39, 78, 89
Fjords, 9
Folklife Institute of Central Kansas, 118,
    120-21
Folk schools, 79, 97-98
Food, 40-41, 69, 77, 87, 88, *89,* 92-93,
    107, 112-13, 114-15, 116, 119, 120-21
Fort Christina, 23, *32-33*
Foss, Laura, 97-98

Galby, Lettie, 70-71
Garbo, Greta, 106
Gjevre, Ole and Maria, *91*
Gods, Nordic, 9
Gold rush (1849), 45, *54, 55*
Graenlendinga Saga, 9
Grundtvig, Nikolai, 79, 112

Hale, Henny, *16-17,* 28-29, 110
Hallberg, Lars G., 46-47
Halldorsson, Jon, 35, 83-84
Handlin, Oscar, 77
Hanhila, Matt, 74

Hannula, Reino, 74-75
Hansen, Sine Nygard, 66-67
Hanson, John, 23
Harald Fairhair, 10
Harlem (New York), 23, 78
Havumaki, Sulo, 107
Heritage, preservation of, *108-17*
Herslev, Andreas Fredericksen, 62
Hill, James J., 45
Hill, Joe, 47, *75*
Hill, Lillie, 56
Hjerpeland, Andreas A., 96
Hofteig, Cecil, 66
Holidays, *12,* 15-16, 80-81, 85-86, 88,
    92, 95, *106,* 107, *108,* 114-15, *116,*
    119, *121*
Holmberg, Rodolph, 21
Homesteaders, *38,* 40-41, 42, 45, *62-71,*
    90-95
Hosmer, Paul, 52
Houkom, A. O., 45
Hovland, Gert Gregoriussen, 45
Hulstrand, Anders, *65*
Humphrey, Hubert H., *6-7,* 107
Humphrey, Hubert H., III, *6-7*

Icelandic Independence Day, 107
Icelandic National League, 79
Immigrant songs, 28
Immigration, *24, 25,* 26-29
    arrival, *36-39,* 40-43
    history, 23-25
    voyage, *30-31*
Industrial Workers of the World (IWW),
    47, 74, *75*
Inner Mission, 79

Jabour, Alan, 121
Jacobsen, Hans, 72
Jamestown, N.Y., *71, 72*
Jansson, Erik, 43
Jarlson, Axel, 13, 19-20, 42, 62-63
Jensen, Jim, 88, 116
Johan, Carl, 64-65
Johanson, Gunnar, 38, 50
Johnsen, Margit, 52
Johnson, Amandus, 108-9
Johnson, Kristina Carlson, 69, 92-93
Johnson, Philip G., 105
John Svan v. *United States* (1908), 47
Jørgensen, Marie, 27-28
J. P. Danielson Company, 72

Kalevala, 11, 79
Kalmar Nyckel (ship), 23, *32*
Kalm, Peter, 33
Kantele, 11, *117*
Kauvala, Martin, 67-68
Kekkonen, Peter, 57, 93
Keyter, Jochem Pietersen, 23
Kjellberg, Isador, 77
Knights of Kalevala, 79
Koren, Elizabeth, 40-41
Koven, Velma Antilla, 60-61
Kuivala, John, 51-52
Kulma, Roberta Christine, 103

Laaksonen, Irja, 28, 39, 89
Labor strike, 47, 56, 74-75

Labor unions, 47, 74-75, 78
Lahti, Aarre, 43, 81-82
Lange, Torben, 30
Language, 25, 77, 87-88, 97, 98-99
Larson, Ellen, 70
Larson, Laurence M., 69-70, 77, 101-2
Larsson, Anders, 85
Lassen, Peter, 45
Law, Eleanor Bystrom, 87-88
Leif Eriksson, 9-10, 107
Lindbergh, Charles, 48-49, 105
Lindgren, Ida, 42, 65
Lind, Jenny, 35
Lind, John, 106
Lindstrom, Walter, 21
Literacy, 14, 78, 91
Literature, 10-11, 70, 86, 105
Ljuskrona, 120, 121
Logging, 46, 48-51, 52, 53
Lönnrot, Elias, 11
Lorensen, Maren, 31, 58-59, 83
Lumppio, Mayme Westervik, 78
Lutheranism, 10, 17, 23, 79, 101-3

Madsen, Frederik, 110, 112
Magnusson, Gudrun Lindal, 112-13
Maki, Alma Emilia, 59
Margrethe, Queen (of Denmark), 11
Martins, Peter, 110
Matanuska Valley, Ala., 46
McGraw, Harriet G., 93
Midsummerfest, 12, 15-16, 95, 106
Milles, Carl, 32
Mining, 25, 46-47, 54-57, 74
Mondale, Walter, 107
Monitor (ship), 45-46
Monson, Jennifer, 21
Mormons, 25, 37, 78, 94, 100-101
Morton, John, 23, 33
Mount Rushmore, S.Dak., 66, 106
Musical instruments, 11, 117, 212
Musicians, 78, 81-82, 91

Neble, Sofus, 19
Nelson, Knute, 106
Nelson, Ozzie and Harriet, 106
Nelson, Ricky and David, 106
Neumann, John, 24
Newspapers, ethnic, 78-79, 91, 114
New Uppsala, Wis., 24
Nielson, Peter, 18
Nilssen, Bergljot Anker, 86-87
Nissen, Christopher, 45
Nordboe, Johannes, 40
Nordic peoples, 9-11
Norse, Tex., 83
Norsk Høstfest, 116
Norwegian Independence Day, 107, 108

Odmark, Elsie, 114
Ohlson, Anna, 59-60, 71
Oldenburg, Claes, 106
Ole Bull, 42
Order of Svithiod, 79
Organizations, 78, 79, 85, 88, 116
Osland, Birger, 30-31
O. W. Siebert Company, 74-75

Pedersen, Lars, 111

Peerson, Cleng, 23-24
Petaluma, Calif., 45
Petersen, Berit, 116-17
Petersen, Julius, 85-86
Petersen, Karl, 72
Petersen, Mourits, 100-101
Peterson, D. A., 26
Peterson, Ellen, 16
Peterson, Minn., 55
Photographers, 53
Pioneers, 37, 38, 90-91
Poets, 86, 185
Politicians, 23, 25, 106-7
Polvi, Isaac, 14-15, 36, 56-57
Ports, 13, 25, 26, 36
Prejudice, 47, 98-99
Printz, Johan, 32
Prospectors, 45, 54, 55
Psalmodikon, 121

Raaen, Aagot, 99
Raaen, Kjersti, 80-81
Racine, Wis., 73, 83, 88, 92
Railroad workers, 54-55, 56
Rasmussen, Martin, 17
Red Scare of 1919-20, 47
Religion, 10, 17, 23, 25, 40, 79, 100-103
Riis, Jacob, 12, 29, 41, 55-56, 105
Robbins, Paula Ivaska, 110-11
Rockne, Knute, 105-6
Rölvaag, Ole, 70, 105
Roosevelt, Franklin D., 105, 106-7
Rosemaling, 117
Rosendahl, John, 82
Runes, 10, 109
Rurik, 10
Rus, 10
Russian Empire, 10, 11, 20, 25
Rynning, Ole, 11, 24

Saarinen, Eero, 105
Saehle, Jannicke, 58
Sagas, 10-11
Salvon, Hilma, 20
Samuelson, Charles, 81
Sandburg, Carl, 86, 105
Sauna, 78, 82-83
Scandinavia
    history of, 9-11
    immigration history of, 23-25
    life in, 12-17
Schmidt, Jens Storm, 54
School, 96-99
Sculptors, 32, 66, 106
Seeburg, Justus P., 105
Seip, Didrik Arup, 20
Sibelius, Jean, 11
Simonette, Huldah Johnson, 96-97
Simonson, Gustav, 52
Sippala, Hannah, 21
Skaeds, 10
Skautkonung, Olaf, 10
Socialism, 47, 78
Social service organizations, 60
Sod homes, 69-70
Soldiers, 45-46
Solvang, Calif., 107, 112
Sommer, Mogens Abraham, 25
Sons of Norway, 79, 116

Sørensen, Rasmus, 24-25
Spanish Fork, Utah, 78, 107
Sports, 76, 82, 87, 105-6, 111
Springer, Charles Christopher, 32-33
Stavanger, Norway, 13, 23
Stefanson, Vilhjalmur, 105
St. Lucia's Day, 116
Strikes, 47, 56, 74-75
St. Urho's Day, 107
Sundvik, Ester, 15-16
Svein Forkbeard, 10
Svendsen, Gro, 65
Swedish Aid Society, 24
Swedish Society, 78
Swenson, Greta, 120
Swenson, Johannes, 26
Swenson, S. M., 45
Synods, 79
Syrjälä, William, 82

Temperance societies, 78, 79, 85
Textile mills, 46
Theater (Finnish), 78, 84, 88, 89
Thingvalla Line, 25, 27, 36
Thomas, W. W., 46
Thompson, Snowshoe, 45
Thoreson, Jon, 45
Thorstad, Erik, 36-37
Timber industry. See Logging
Turpeinen, Viola, 82

Union of Kalmar, 11
Unionus, Gustaf, 24, 35

Väänänen-Jensen, Inkeri, 82-83, 117
Vasa Order of America, 79
Veblen, Thorstein, 105
Viking Order, 78
Vikings, 9-10, 109
Vinland, 9

Waerenskjold, Elise Amalie, 64
Walters, Thorstina, 13, 41-42, 68-69, 91-92, 113-14
Warren, Earl, 106, 109
Washington Island, Mich., 25, 51
Weddings, 85-86, 95
Wermelin, Atterdag, 72-73
Wiback, Stina, 58
Wickman, Eric, 105
Wickmann, William, 25
William the Conqueror, 10
Wilmington, Del., 23, 32
Wilse, Anders, 53
Wilson, Woodrow, 47
Winter War, 11, 110-11
Wirtanen, Donald G., 98-99
Wobblies, 47, 74, 75
Women
    immigrants, 24, 25, 41, 46
    work of, 16, 46, 50-51, 52, 56, 58-61, 64, 67, 80, 91-92
World War I, 47, 74
Writers, 70, 86, 105

Yost, Gretchen, 43

Zaharias, Mildred "Babe" Didrikson, 93-94, 106

ACKNOWLEDGMENTS

In the course of our research, we met in person, and via telephone or the Internet, many people who generously contributed their time, personal photographs, and memories to this book. We are deeply grateful to Eleanor Law, Jim Jensen, Velma Doby of the Finnish Family History Project, Berit Petersen, Elsie Tenney, Laila Suomela, Leola Josefson, Scotty Sapiro, John T. Erickson, Joann Laitinen Hall, Sally Roesch Wagner, Kirk Wiebe, and Neal D. and Ferne Larson Williams.

Our special thanks for the wonderful afternoon we spent with Ida Gurney and all the other hospitable and generous people at the Finn Hall in South Paris, Maine, and to Nancy Austin, who very kindly gathered photographs for us in the Worcester, Massachusetts, area. Our gratitude and admiration to Reino Hannula, for his contributions to the preservation of Finnish American culture through his wonderful publication *Finn Heritage*.

Thanks also to the dozens of others who helped us in so many ways to assemble this book: Alan Barnett of the Utah State Historical Society; Henning Bender of the Danish Emigration Archives; Hans Berggreen of Det Kongelige Bibliotek, Copenhagen; Suzen Brasile and Jackie Traylor of the Solvang (Calif.) Conference and Visitors Bureau; Forrest Brown and Ruth Hanald Crane of the Norwegian-American Historical Association; Diane Bruce of the Institute of Texan Cultures; Carrie Buck of the Goodhue County Historical Society; John E. Bye, Pam Johnson, and Richard W. Bovard of the North Dakota Institute for Regional Studies; Theresa B. Davitt of the Worcester Historical Museum; Pam Davy and Chester Reiten, of Hostfest; Tara Deal and Nancy Toff, our editors, who have now contributed their knowledge, patience, and tenacity to 10 books in this series; Sirkku Dölle of the Finnish National Museum; Jeffrey S. Dosik and Barry Moreno of the Ellis Island National Monument; Mario M. Einaudi of the Arizona Historical Society; Richard Engeman and Kristin Kinsey of the Allen Library at the University of Washington; Thomas Featherstone of the Walter P. Reuther Library; Marianne Forssblad and Lisa Hill-Festa of the Nordic Heritage Museum; Arlene M. Fults of the Runestone Museum; Nelson S. Gerrard of Saga Publications and Research; Marja-Leena Hänninen of the National Board of Antiquities, Helsinki, Finland; Mrs. Gunn Hidle of the Norwegian Emigration Center; Christina Johansson and Jill Seaholm of the Swenson Swedish Immigration Research Center; Andy Kraushaar and David Benjamin of the State Historical Society of Wisconsin; Charles Langton of the Vesterheim Norwegian-American Museum; Birgit Flemming Larsen of the Danes Worldwide Archives; Sylvia Lobb of the Fenton Historical Society; Barbara Lund-Jones of the Danish Immigrant Museum; Staughton and Alice Lynd; Mary McCoy of the Delaware Swedish Colonial Society; Carolyn J. Marr of the Museum of History and Industry; Kay Masters of the MTU Archives and Copper Country Historical Collections at Michigan Technological University; Lori Merrill and Carrie Floto of the Bishop Hill Heritage Association; Michael M. Miller, of the Germans from Russia Heritage Collection; Becky Morford of the Mount Rushmore National Memorial; I. J. Müller of the Norsk Folkemuseum; Steve Nielson of the Minnesota Historical Society; Susan Otto of the Milwaukee Public Museum; Stefan Valur Palsson of Ljósmyndasafn Reykjavíkborgar; Holger Munchaus Petersen; Alf Petesson of the Hoganås Museum; Janet E. Rasmussen; Timo Riippa and Joel Wurl of the Immigration History Research Center at the University of Minnesota; Kirsten Ringdahl of the Scandinavian Immigrant Experience Collection at Pacific Lutheran University; June Sampson, Marilee Christensen, Barbara Hansen, and Todd Strand of the State Historical Society of North Dakota; Valerie Sauers, for her inspired work in designing this book; Sigurdur B. Sigurdsson; Judith Simonsen of the Milwaukee County Historical Society; Irene A. Stachura of the National Maritime Museum; Christie K. Stanley of the Kansas State Historical Society; Niels Peter Stilling of the Søllerød Museum; Petur Thorsteinsson, of the Icelandic Embassy; Mikki Tint and Mrs. Cecil Housel of the Oregon Historical Society; Erica Schoenhals Toland of the San Francisco Maritime National Historical Park; Ib Varnild of the National Museum of Denmark; and Katherine Wyatt of the Nebraska State Historical Society.

Finally, we want to express our heartfelt gratitude to Mark and Mardel Esping for their contributions and advice, as well as for their generosity in sharing with us their memories and personal family albums. Through the tireless and unselfish efforts of the Espings—and people like them throughout the nation—the immensely rich heritage of all Americans is being treasured and preserved for future generations. It has been our privilege to know them and to help others enjoy their work.

ABOUT THE AUTHORS

Dorothy and Thomas Hoobler have published more than 60 books for children and young adults, including *Margaret Mead: A Life in Science; Vietnam: Why We Fought; Showa: The Age of Hirohito; Buddhism;* and *Japanese Portraits.* Their works have been honored by the Society for School Librarians International, the Library of Congress, the New York Public Library, the National Council for Social Studies, and *Best Books for Children,* among other organizations and publications. The Hooblers have also written several volumes of historical fiction for children, including *Next Stop Freedom, Frontier Diary, The Summer of Dreams,* and *Treasure in the Stream.* Dorothy Hoobler received her master's degree in American history from New York University and worked as a textbook editor before becoming a full-time free-lance editor and writer. Thomas Hoobler received his master's degree in education from Xavier University and has worked as a teacher and textbook editor.

FOSSIL RIDGE PUBLIC LIBRARY DISTRICT
Braidwood, IL 60408